The British Book
of
Spells and Charms

D1569361

WHO SO BEARS THIS
SIGN ADOUT HIM, LET
HIM FEAR NO ONE, BUT
FEAR GOD.

The British Book
of
Spells & Charms

*A Compilation
of Traditional Folk Magic*

Graham King
*past curator of
The Museum of Witchcraft*

© 2014-2015 Graham King

First printed in paperback June 2016

ISBN 978-1-909602-17-5

All rights reserved.
No part of this publication may be reproduced,
stored within a retrieval system or transmitted in any
form or by any means, electronic,
mechanical, photocopying, scanning, recording or
otherwise, without the prior written permission of
the author and the publisher.

Any practices or substances described within this
publication are presented as items of interest. The
author and publisher accept no responsibility for any
results arising from their enactment or use. Readers
are self-responsible for their actions.

Published by Troy Books
www.troybooks.co.uk

Troy Books Publishing
BM Box 8003
London WC1N 3XX

Image Credits & Acknowledgements

With thanks to: The Museum of Witchcraft,
John Hooper, Jane Cox, Gemma Gary,
Scarborough Museum, The Cornwall Records
Office, The National Library of Wales, Bill
Lovett and Jeannet Richel.

Special thanks to Kerriann Godwin and the
Museum of Witchcraft team.

To the memory of
Michael Howard
(1948 - 2015)
a wise man

Contents

Good Luck

The Author

I was born in 1954 in the south of England and was educated in one of the country's first comprehensive schools. After serving an apprenticeship in the Royal Air Force, where I studied radio communications and electronics, my career continued in various technical roles, notably as the managing director of Gratek Ltd. This was a company that designed and manufactured specialist cameras for recording old and rare books and documents. The company's customers included national libraries and record offices in more than fifty countries around the world.

Soon after leaving school I developed a keen interest in traditional folk music and clearly remember the spine tingling effect of hearing two chaps singing in a pub near Locking, in Somerset, where I was stationed in the RAF in the 1970s. Our indigenous, ancient songs, music and harmony can be totally magical – they can transform a mood instantly and place the listener in a different time and place.

Some years later, I joined Kirtlington Morris and started dancing (badly) that wonderful Cotswold tradition. Again the magic of time and place affected me deeply – it was important to dance the dances of the villages and our country – to connect with the spirits of place and our ancestors. There were villagers who truly believed that crop growth would be hindered if the dance didn't take place. This is folk magic at it purest. Morris dancing isn't performed simply to entertain, or just because it's fun, it is done because it is vital! To dance the Morris is to cast a spell! My love of English traditions grew into a passion.

Spells, charms and magic are as much a part of British folk culture as dancing around the maypole, singing old songs in the pub and playing cricket. My interest in folk magic increased drastically after I discovered that charms often worked! I remember a close friend telling me how much he and his wife wanted children. 'You know about magic', he said, 'can you do a spell for us?' After a long discussion, and a lot of thought, I agreed to give it a go. I spent a few days preparing then waited for the dark of the moon. On my own in the woods, I performed my secret ritual – after nine months my friends delivered a fine and healthy son into the world. I am not sure who was most surprised but since that day I totally believe that spells can work!

In 1996, after a particularly gruelling business trip to America, I went walking on the Pewsey Downs seeking to rid myself of some of the stress of running a business. Wandering through the English countryside has always been one of my most effective medications. After a short walk, I stumbled across a group of travellers who had set up camp in traditional benders (tents made from hazel hoops and tarpaulins). The youngsters were playing instruments, singing and dancing around a fire. I was offered and accepted a cup of hot nettle and sage tea and that moment sowed a seed that was to change my life. The travellers explained that they were gathering to celebrate the ancient Tan Hill Fair, and later they danced naked on the hillside as the sun set, and their pure, un-amplified music rolled across the ancient landscape. Magic!

Within a few days I had decided that the corporate lifestyle was not for me. I told my colleagues of my decision to sell my company, car, and pretty thatched cottage – I put them all on the market. Soon after this, a friend showed me a magazine article about the Museum of Witchcraft in Boscastle which, due to the owner's age and imminent retirement, was up for sale. 'You should buy that', suggested the friend, and the rest is history.

In an act of magic I literally burnt my suits and ties and set off on foot from Hampshire. I was ridding myself of the need to look smart and go to business meetings. I set out on a long new path and walked the 200 odd miles to the north coast of Cornwall where, at midnight on the 31st October 1996, I purchased The Museum of Witchcraft. I had decided to make a pilgrimage of it and leave the old corporate word behind.

With a lot of help from friends, the Museum was gradually transformed from a fascinating but rather run-down and dated attraction into one of the most popular museums in Cornwall.

Living on the coast in Boscastle, I offered my services to HM Coastguards as I had some skills in radio communications learnt in the RAF. My offer was accepted and I am very proud of the 10 years I served as an auxiliary Coastguard. In the terrible floods that devastated Boscastle in the summer of 2004, I raised the alert that led to a massive rescue operation saving hundreds of lives and, as Deputy Station Officer, I was awarded the Chief Coastguard Commendation for my small part in the remarkable rescue. I met Prince Charles on a couple of occasions, and even had a brief chat with the Queen in Buckingham Palace!

In 2011, the Museum of Witchcraft celebrated its 50th year in Boscastle and 60 years since it first opened on the Isle of Man.

Magic keeps happening in Boscastle, especially around the Museum. I am often asked to 'go and ask that in front of the Museum', for every request I make there seem to come true. I must remember to stand outside the Museum and wish that this book is a success!

Introduction

Rain rain, go away,
Come again another day.

Who in England has not chanted this old charm? As I sit in my office above The Museum of Witchcraft on this October evening, I utter the words and wish with all my heart that the spell will work so that I can pop down to the pub for a pint without getting soaked.

We see, hear, and use spells and charms surprisingly often, but seldom do we recognise them for what they are. Spells and charms were, or should I say are, for every day use. They are to cure toothache, to stop bleeding, to find out who your lover will be, or to discover who stole your possessions.

Walk through any country village today and you will find cottages with a horseshoe prominently displayed on the front door.

The residents might not profess to believe in magic but, nevertheless, they have a magical charm nailed to their door to bring them luck and protect them from ill. The writer of a satirical article in *'The World'* in 1776 offered the following advice:

> *To secure yourself against the enchantments of witches, especially if you are a person of fashion and have never been taught the Lord's Prayer, the only method I know of is to nail a horseshoe upon the threshold. This I can affirm to be of the greatest efficacy, insomuch that I have taken notice of many a little cottage in the country with a horseshoe at its door where gaming, extravagance, Jacobitism, and all the catalogue of witchcrafts have been totally unknown.*

These old magical ways also survive in folk song, in local customs, and in every day life, and I believe that we are all the better for it. We are also lucky that so much of our magical folklore has been preserved and collected. I am especially fortunate to have The Museum of Witchcraft library to hand, with its wealth of esoteric material including many books and documents that contain spells and charms.

These spells and charms were collected in the countryside, as well as in urban areas. In the 1920s, folklorist Edward Lovett mixed with the street traders and collected their charms, good luck trinkets and stories. He confirms that wearing amulets was as popular in early 20th century London as it was in the 16th Century. In his 1925 book *'Magic in Modern London'* he wrote:

> *...my own experience is that, at any rate for the seeker after amulets, there is no better hunting ground than the hawker's handbarrow in the poorest parts of slums of such dense aggregations of people as London, Rome, and Naples.*[1]

Referring to the London street traders Lovett confirmed:

---

1. Lovett, Edward. *Magic in Modern London*, 1925.

I am much surprised to find how much they know as to the reasons for carrying certain amulets.[2]

Following in Lovett's footsteps today reveals that not much has changed. Many of the small back street shops have a plastic, nodding cat close to the till or in the window. This Maneki-Neko is a Japanese magical charm to ensure prosperity. Chinese restaurants display their red lanterns for similar reasons, and it is not difficult to find a tarot reader or astrologer in 21st Century London.

In 1951, Cecil Williamson opened The Museum of Witchcraft on the Isle of Man. Williamson had been collecting spells, charms and magical knowledge for many years along with the wands, cauldrons, herbs and other paraphernalia that make up a witch's tool kit. He became somewhat of an expert in magical matters and, during the Second World War, his occult knowledge was used by the British secret services. He was sent to Germany

2. *Ibid*

to gather information on occultists, and his expertise was used to predict how and when the occult influenced Nazi party planned offensives.

But Williamson was drawn to the village wise women, or 'wayside witches' as he used to call them. He did collect the regalia and artefacts used by occultists and ritual magicians, but it was the folk magic of the common person that fascinated him most. Williamson realised it was a myth that village witches were poorly educated and illiterate. The village wise woman often used the same reference books as the ritual magicians, and the amulets and talismans drawn by the charmer in the country were the same as those used by elite and secret occult societies.

After his death in 1999, I began to realise that not only had Williamson understood the old ways of magic, but that he used them too. When helping his family to clear out his house, I found a large scrying mirror set on an easel in his study and clearly positioned for regular use. This was a 'dark mirror' – one that does not fully reflect. It is used rather like a gypsy's crystal ball; by focusing the eye just behind the surface until, with time and practice, images and spirits appear. I also found various dated talismans amongst his private papers that clearly demonstrated that he was practicing magic, not just collecting.

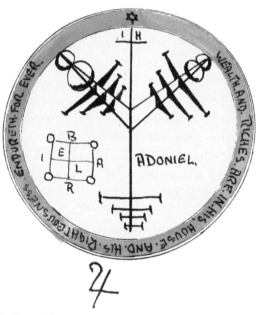

The Fourth Pentacle of Jupiter, drawn by Cecil Williamson.
The Museum of Witchcraft (No. 1898)

While reading the large archive of Williamson letters, I began to get a feeling for the sort of spells, charms and methodology that he found most effective. Very often, it was a case of repeating a simple phrase over and over again, sometimes for up to an hour at a time. *'Bulstrode away, Bulstrode away, Bulstrode away'*, he chanted to stop a bully by that name returning to school after the summer holidays. He also liked to use the wind and smoke to deliver and receive spells. His methods included flying a kite into the smoke from a chimney to capture the 'essence' of the household for magic making. Also, he would light a smoky fire under a swing and rock to and fro in the smoke whilst repeating his charms and working his magic. His documents describe similar techniques used to resolve many different problems, from preventing Hitler invading England, to stopping dogs leaving a mess on tourist beaches. Today, the Museum of Witchcraft in Boscastle is crammed full of magical items that Cecil Williamson had gathered through his long and interesting life. This book is shaped by that collection.

I do hope the act of recording these spells in writing does not remove their effectiveness, for there is a tradition in many regions that they can only be conveyed verbally. When the Rev. R.S. Hawker asked a Cornish charmer if he could document his spells, he was told that 'their virtue would be utterly destroyed when he was gone, by their being put into ink.'[3]

There are also traditions that specify that only men can pass charms to women, and women must pass them on to men. However, as usual when dealing with magic, there are many contradictory regional customs. Some dictate that charms can only pass from male to male or female to female, and even some that say they must never be spoken, only written. Also, always remember not to thank the spell-caster as it is a widespread belief that a charm will not work if the recipient says 'please' or 'thank you' to the charmer.

---

3. *The Cornish Antiquary*. Oakmagic, 2002

When confronted with a large collection of old spells, it becomes clear that they are flexible and adaptable. One spell can be adapted to suit different situations, and most popular spells and charms have been changed or modified over time to cater for individual requirements. If a spell called upon a saint or god that the spell-caster felt uncomfortable with, it was simply changed. Or, if a spell to suit a particular situation was not known, a similar one was borrowed and modified to suit. Our ancestors have been doing this for hundreds, if not thousands of years, and the tradition continues.

This is the nature of spells and charms: they pass from person to person, generation to generation, and much like old folk songs or antique furniture, they gather regional and personal variations, a patina that often improves with age. The literal meanings and pronunciation of words change, the ingredients, the saints' names and the language all change, but over the years the magical essence of the spell survives. I always say that if you can fully understand the

words of a folk song it is probably not
very old. Over generations, words are
misheard, misremembered and changed,
yet the essence of the song survives. The
same is true of spells and charms. It is
not important that a spell or charm is
nonsensical. Spells do not have to make
sense, and indeed many seem deliberately
unintelligible, such as the following which
is part of a spell to restore lost money:

> *Flibberty, gibberty, flasky flum*
> *Calafac, tarada, lara, wagra wum.*
> *Hooky, maroosky, whatever's the sum.*[4]

I have not attempted to compile a
comprehensive collection of spells
and charms in this book, but I have
endeavoured to present a selection that
demonstrate their development, variety
and unique beauty.

In this work I humbly follow in the
footsteps of many other worthy 'charm-
stealers', including Cecil Williamson and
many of my friends. Indeed, almost all

4. Hewett, Sarah. *Nummits & Crummits,* 1900

of the spells and charms quoted in the following pages have been published before, and I am merely passing them on. The authors of the books and documents from which I have accumulated this collection acquired their charms from others, and likewise those before them.

Spells and charms add colour and sparkle to life, not to mention magic, and we can never have too much magic in our lives!

Key & cord charm image from the Richel Collection
Museum of Witchcraft (No. R/5/715)

What is a Spell or Charm?

Dictionaries tell us that spells are a form of spoken words that contain, or are thought to contain, magical power. Likewise, a charm is an object or saying that is thought to contain similar power. In popular usage, both words have become interchangeable when referring to spoken or written magical expressions. A better definition of a spell might be 'a set of actions and/or words intended to bring about a change or revelation'. The change might be to cure an illness, improve the weather or simply bring good luck. The 'revelation' is usually to show the location of a lost object, or to show the identity of a future lover.

All hail new moon, all hail to thee
I prithee good moon, reveal to me
This night who shall my true love be:
Who he is and what he wears,
And what he does for months and years.[1]

A charm can simply be a physical object, like a hagstone (a holed stone), that has naturally or magically been imbued with a magical power. But often spells and charms are rather more complicated. They may, for example, require ritual or actions from the spell-caster, like visiting a particular place at a specific time or moon phase, by sowing seeds, turning clockwise three times or drawing a magic circle on the floor.

Go to the four cross-roads to-night, all alone, and just as the clock strikes twelve, turn yourself about three times and drive a tenpenny nail into the ground up to the head, and walk away from the place backwards before the clock is done striking, and you will miss the ague; but the next person who passes over the nail will take it in your stead.[2]

---

1. Roper, Jonathan. *English Verbal Charms*, p. 136
2. Glyde, John. *The New Suffolk Garland*, 1866

Items to bring the bearer luck or protection from evil are sometimes referred to as amulets and are often carried or worn. An object made, usually written or engraved, for a specific magical purpose is called a talisman (the frontispiece to this book is an old talisman). Today, the words 'amulet', 'talisman' and 'charm' are often interchanged. Spells and charms were usually written or made by a witch, wise woman or other practitioner of the magic arts but many have entered popular culture, and occasionally this ancient folk magic can be recognised in everyday sayings, nursery rhymes, and traditional customs and ceremonies.

Something old
Something new
Something borrowed
Something blue.
(to ensure good fortune to a bride.)

Many charms have a poetic quality and have to be repeated several times, in full or in part, to make them effective. Repetition usually happens three or nine times and odd numbers seem to have a special significance.

> *Matthew, Mark, Luke, and John,*
> *The bed be blessed that I lye on.*
> (To be said three times on going to bed, to protect the sleeper overnight.)

Written charms often have a symmetrical quality, either building or diminishing on paper, or including a magic square, pentacle, or other magic symbol.

```
ABRACADABRA
ABRACADABR
ABRACADAB
ABRACADA
ABRACAD
ABRACA
ABRAC
ABRA
ABR
AB
A
```

'Sympathetic magic' is common in both spells and charms. For example, a spider might be placed in a pouch to cure a sore throat; the pouch would be worn around the neck of the patient and when the spider stops wriggling (i.e. it dies), the tickling throat would also disappear. This is not particularly sympathetic to the spider though who, through imitation, took on the ailment. This magical transference of a problem from one person to another or to an animal or plant is also common.

As this bean-shell rots away,
So my wart soon shall decay.[3]

So what makes a good charm or spell? I am not sure that it is possible to define the formula for a perfect charm or spell, but we can start by looking at the more common physical 'ingredients', some of which seem to have an enduring attraction to spell-makers and magicians. The toad (sometimes a frog is substituted) is, for example, the prime ingredient in many an old spell and charm. In the early Roman Empire, Pliny the Elder observed that

---

3. Roper, Jonathan. *English Verbal Charms,* p. 138

there was a red toad that lived in briars and brambles that is *'full of sorceries'*, and if a little bone from the toad's left side is cast into water, it will make the water very hot. The same bone could apparently restrain the rage of dogs and procure their love, and when put in a drink would also *'stirreth up lust'*. The little bone from the right side of the toad *'makes hot water cold, and that it can never be hot again, unless that be taken out, also it is said to cure quartanes if it be bound to the sick in a snake's skin, as also all other fevers, and restrain love, and lust. And that the spleen and heart is an effectual remedy against the poisons of the said Toad.'*

A stone found in the head of a toad was once prized for its magical properties and sometimes mounted in rings or carried in charm bags as amulets. An example of a toad stone ring can be viewed in the Victoria and Albert Museum in London.

To make sure that your toadstone is the real thing, you are advised to *'... holde the stone before a Tode, so that he may see it; and, if it be a right and true stone, the Tode will leape towarde it.'* [4]

Acquiring Toad Stones from Hortus Sanitatis 1490

Indeed, the humble toad seems to have many magical properties. In East Anglia and other areas, bread (the host) stolen from a church during Holy Communion is fed to a toad as part of an elaborate witchcraft initiation ritual.[5]

Rowan wood and berries are popular ingredients, as are pieces of red thread, whole cats, parts of cats, bottles, knots in rope, blood, and bones.

4. Brant, John. *Observations on Popular Antiquities*, 1842

5. *Devonshire Association Folk-Lore Transactions*, 1907

Take the gall of a cat and hen's fat,
Mixing them together.
Put this on your eyes and you will
See things which are invisible to others.[6]

Spells and charms sometimes contain words that are considered to be important, or to have magical properties; words of power. We all know 'Abracadabra', but other popular ones include *'Adonai'*, *'AGLA'*, *'Elohim'* and *'Tetragrammaton'*. Some of these words are seemingly nonsensical, while others are corruptions of words from various languages. It is thought that the mere act of writing these words is in itself magical, and in 1596 the dramatist Thomas Lodge wrote:

'Bring him but a table of lead, with Crosses and Adonai or Elohim written on it, he thinks it will heal the Ague.' [7]

Many of these special words are popular in written charms but uncommon in

---

6. The Museum of Witchcraft Library & Archives

7. Brant, John. *Observations on Popular Antiquities*, 1842

verbal charms. *'AGLA'* for example is one of the most common words in written talismans and amulets, but is not found mentioned in any of the spoken charms that I have found. The word *'AGLA'* is an acronym for the Qabbalistic expression, Atah Gibor Le-olam Adonai, 'Thou, O Lord, are mighty forever', and is often considered to be a magical name for God, the divine name, the incommunicable name, or the perfect word.

Magic is sometimes defined as the art of obtaining a desired result through will or special power, and a spell or charm is the means by which that magical deed is performed. So could the same definition not also apply to a prayer, or indeed a thought? If we pray for a good exam result, are we not using magic? When we wish someone a good day or *bon voyage,* aren't we trying to influence an outcome by vocalising it?

In 1681, Glanvill tells us that witches would say *'merry meet, merry part'* [8] as they

---

8. Glanvill. *Saducismus Trimphatus,* 1681

parted after a coven meeting. I suspect that this was more than just a pleasant farewell – that it is, in itself, a charm.

In his book *'Satan's Invisible World Discovered'* (1685), George Sinclair tells us *'Charming is much practised by the Pope, and the Romish Church. Their whole form of religion both in private and in public consists of Charms of all sorts.'* One definition says that a prayer calls for direct communication with God or a higher power to obtain a desired outcome, whereas a spell relies on the magical skill or power of the perpetrator. But this could be questioned:

> *Christ was born in Bethlehem*
> *Baptised in the river Jordan*
> *There he digg'd a well*
> *And turn'd the water against the hill,*
> *So shall thy blood stand still!*
> *In the name of the Father, Son,*
> *and Holy Ghost.*[9]

9. Roper, Jonathan. *English Verbal Charms*, p. 107

Is this common and very old charm (to stop bleeding) a spell or a prayer? Or is it both? Some ancient spells that evoked the powers of old Gods have been Christianised to incorporate a saint or Christ. One has to ponder which would have worked best, a spell that called upon the power of the ancient god Woden, or one that used Christ? And would the faith or beliefs of the person performing the invocation affect the outcome of the spell? You will notice that many of the spells and charms in this book have a Christian flavour, mentioning Saints, Christ or the Holy Trinity:

Mary mild has burnt her child
By the sparking of the fire
Out fire
In frost
In the name of the father, son,
and Holy Ghost
Amen Amen Amen.[10]
  (To heal a burn)

---

10. Roper, Jonathan. *English Verbal Charms*, p. 122

The origin of some of these spells could well predate the Christian religion, and it is entirely possible that variants of some of the spells will outlast that religion. It is, however, very interesting to note that few, if any, of these spells would ever have been acceptable within the Christian church.

This for example is the healing prayer of Agnes Sampson (followed by the modern translation), who was famously tried for witchcraft in North Berwick in 1590:

All kindes of illis that ewir may be,
In Chrystis name I coniure ye,
In coniure ye baith mair and les,
With all the vertewis of the mes,
Any rycht sa be the naillis sa,
That naillith Jesus and no ma;
And rycht sa be the samin blude,
That raikit owir the ruithfull rude,
Furth of the flesch and of the bane,
And in the urd and in the stane.
I coniure ye in Godis name.[11]

---

11. Pitcairn. *Criminal Trials in Scotland*, 1833

All kinds of ills that ever may be,
In Christ's name I conjure ye,
I conjure you both more and less,
With all the virtues of the mass,
And right so by the nails so,
That naileth Jesus and no more;
And right so by the same blood,
Than ran over the rueful cross,
Forth of [from] *the flesh and of the bone,*
And in the earth and in the stone,
I conjure you in God's name.

Various Christian practices are so 'witchy' that if they were not taking place in a Christian shrine or church, they would certainly be frowned upon by The Church. The leaving of votive charms in shrines is one such practice. Offerings may be left to a saint or divinity to help attain their assistance or favour. These offerings often take the form of wax or metal effigies of people, human limbs, or various other artefacts.

Imagine that you have hurt your leg after a fall and that you visit a local woman known for her healing skills. After a short consultation she makes a wax effigy of your leg and utters strange incantations over it, maybe she incorporates some of your hair into the wax. She then accompanies you to a local healing shrine, where the wax leg is placed in front of a saint's statue. Candles are lit, incense wafted, more prayers and incantations offered and the magic is done. The wise woman now sends you home, tells you to put your feet up and take it easy for a day or two and to say your prayers; her magic, aided by your saint will now heal your leg. This combination of witchcraft, Christianity and practicality was once common and widespread, and is still practiced in various forms throughout the world. This is a classic form of sympathetic magic and witchcraft, but it is taking place in a church.

Votive offerings are also sometimes left in shrines to demonstrate the donor's gratitude to a saint for services rendered, maybe for surviving a shipwreck or the safe delivery of a child. It's always best to remain in the saint's good books – you never know when you will need him or her next!

The practice of leaving offerings to attract the help of supernatural forces goes back to at least Neolithic times when polished axe heads were deliberately deposited in special sites. Later, bronze spearheads and high quality swords and pins were ritually placed in sacred rivers, springs or wells. It is particularly interesting to note that, prior to placement, these items were often bent or rendered useless, a practice that continued in various forms into modern times. Seventeenth century witch bottles (see pages 206 & 207) often contain bent pins, and some spells that foretell your future love involve floating bent pins in holy wells.

In love magic, pins were sometimes used to 'prick the heart' of a poppet (doll) made in the image of the one you wanted to marry. They were also floated on wood or leaves in holy wells in an attempt to divine who your future lover would be. I wonder if throwing away a pin on a wedding day to ensure good luck is also connected to these rituals?

There is an old tradition in spell craft, as with most things in life, that the more you put into a spell the more you will get out of it or the better it will work. Perhaps the act of destroying or sacrificing something valuable, like a sword or pin (for pins were once valuable), improves the effectiveness of the spell. The Chinese tradition of burning imitation paper money may well also be related to this universal folk magic.

So, next time you toss a coin into a wishing well, remember that you are casting a spell that is part of an ancient and ongoing tradition; that of leaving offerings or a sacrifice in exchange for a magical favour from a deity.

My favourite, and indeed some of the most rare spells and charms, are intended to be sung. The magical quality of this cloth consecration charm from the Hebrides is still evident in this translation from the Gaelic. Deosil means sun-wise or clockwise:

Deosil turn once }	
Deosil turn twice }	suiting the actions
Deosil turn thrice }	to the words

The Sun is to the Western sea
Mankind to the trinity
In each deed for aye and aye
And in solace
The blessings of the Lord upon this cloth
May heroes wear it and enjoy it
By sea
By land
In the changes of mighty waves
One song on it!
Two songs on it!
Three songs on it!
May there be sewed to it nothing
But the music and laughter of maidens
Honey kisses of fair ones
And singing ones
And that suficeth![12]

The concept of sewing kisses, laughter and music into a garment is simply beautiful, and I for one would love to wear a garment that had been blessed with this exquisite charm.

---

12. Collected by M. Kennedy-Fraser & K. Macleod, published 1909

Mano Cornuto or horned hand
Museum of Witchcraft (No. 743)

Good Luck & Protection Charms

*Spells and Charms to Ensure Good Fortune
and Protection from Evil*

Most people, at some time in their lives, have owned or used a good luck charm. Usually these charms are in the form of an amulet that is carried around with them; this might be a lucky coin or a special stone kept in one's pocket. For others, it might be a magical talisman, sigil or text written on virgin parchment, kept in a secret place, or in a pouch suspended around the neck.

These amulets often serve a double purpose, to attract good luck and to protect from misfortune. Attracting good luck must offer protection from bad luck, for example a house with good luck will not be burgled, and protection from evil must attract good luck – a house that is never burgled must have good luck. Hence the similarity of protection charms and good luck charms. There is however a magical tradition that a specific spell for a specific problem will be more efficacious than a general spell. If you need to protect your cattle from being bewitched, it would be better to use a spell designed for that purpose than to carry a rabbit's foot for general good luck.

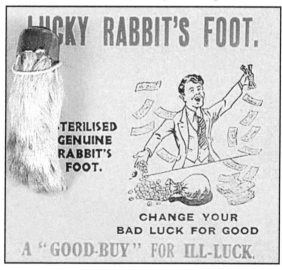

Advertisement from 1942. Author's collection

Protection charms abound in rural Britain. Cottages have horseshoes nailed to their front doors, charms and spells hidden above and below their thresholds, dead cats secreted in their walls, and witch bottles and pinned animal hearts in their chimneys. But the horseshoe is the king of protection charms. There is nothing that will better guarantee good fortune for a house and household than to find an old horseshoe in a field and nail it to your front door. As Thomas Q. Couch said in 1855: *'There are few farmhouses without it, and scarcely a boat or vessel put to sea without this talisman'*. In 1889, Robert Lawrence confirms that: *'There are comparatively few small vessels laden with wood, fruit, vegetables, or other merchandise, sailing between Baltic Sea ports, upon whose foremast, or elsewhere upon deck, horse-shoes are not nailed.'*[1] Indeed, even Lord Horatio Nelson had a horseshoe nailed to the mast of his flagship HMS Victory to ensure the wellbeing of ship and crew.

---

1. Lawrence, Robert. *The Magic Of The Horse-Shoe,* 1889

Which way up should a horseshoe be attached for best results? In Derbyshire we are told to *'...drive a horseshoe, prongs upward, between two flag-stones near the door.....so placed, the luck cannot spill out.'* [2]

However, traditions vary throughout the country. In general, it is thought that pointing the ends upwards will hold in the luck, and ends down will keep evil out – points up to attract good fortune, and points down to protect from evil. In his excellent book 'The Magic of the Horse-Shoe', Robert Means Lawrence advises:

Farmers may well take heed how they nail up horseshoes over the doors of their barns. To obtain the best results, it would seem advisable to place a pair of these useful articles on each farm building, one with the points upward, the other reversed; for in this way they may not only hope to win Fortune's smiles, but also to keep all witches and unfriendly spirits at a respectful distance.

---

2. Lawrence, Robert. *The Magic Of The Horse-Shoe,* 1889

It is said that demons and evil spirits cannot pass a horseshoe:

Laugh if you will, who imps nor devils fear,
Whom death appalls not, phantoms come not near;
Along whose nerves no quick vibrations dart,
As teeming twilight's shadowy offspring start;
Not yours to feel the joy with which I flew
To snatch the rusty, worn, but lucky shoe.
Oft have I heard them chattering at my door,
The hags whose dances beat the shrinking moor;
Oft have I sprung from nightmare-haunted rest,
And gasped an oro from my panting breast,
As forms that vanished ere the half-shut eye
With fright could open, from their revels fly.
Henceforth, good horse-shoe, vain shall be their ride
Their spells are baffled and their rage defied.[3]

We partake of a powerful and ancient protection ritual every time we 'touch wood' or 'knock on wood' three times, or even when we buy 'lucky' white heather from a gypsy. These seemingly simple old charms have survived for hundreds if not thousands of years and have become folk

3. Ibid.

customs. To be sure your luck will last when seeing a lone magpie – 'the devil's bird' – always greet it with *'Good Morning Mr Magpie!'* Or, if in Staffordshire, you must spit towards the bird saying 'devil, devil, I defy thee!'[4] Likewise, if you stumble across a four leafed clover, you must complete the magic by chanting:

*One leaf for fame
And one for wealth,
And one for a faithful lover,
one to bring you glorious health,
And all are in a four-leafed clover.*[5]

Or, when you see the first star of the night, you must make a wish and say out loud:

*Star light, star bright,
First star that I see tonight
I wish I may, I wish I might,
Have the wish I wish tonight.*[6]

4. Hole, Christina. *English Folklore*, 1940

5. Thomas & Pavit. *The Book of Talismans & Zodiacal Gems*, 1914

6. The Museum of Witchcraft Library & Archives

Whilst some these charms have lasted for centuries, others fall in and out of fashion – possibly the best example is the swastika that was, prior to its misuse in the Second World War, one of the most popular good luck charms in Britain.

Early 20th Century Postcard. Museum of Witchcraft (No. 1537)

The swastika symbol is thought to represent the Sun which is universally linked with good fortune.

During the First World War, British soldiers were often given a 'Fums Up' or 'Touchwood' doll for luck and protection in the trenches. These tiny dolls incorporated many classic good luck motifs (the image of a new born baby has always been considered lucky).

When Romans fought
With sword and knife
The sign Fums Up
Meant spare his life.[7]

The doll's arms are articulated and can swivel up to touch the wooden head. The thumbs on the doll stick out in the classic 'thumbs up' gesture, on the head is a four-leaved clover, and on its heels are 'cupid's wings'.

A Fums Up doll from the Museum of Witchcraft collection also includes a 'poem' in the accompanying leaflet:

---

7. From leaflet accompanying a 'Fums Up' doll

For Luck
Behold in me
The birth of luck,
Two charms combined
TOUCHWOOD-FUMSUP
My head is made
Of wood most rare,
My thumbs turn up
To touch me there.
To speed my feet
They've Cupid's wings;
They'll help true love
'Moungst other things,
Proverbial is
My power to bring
Good luck to you
In everything.
I'll bring good luck
To all away-
Just send me to
A friend to-day.

A 'Fums Up' Charm
Museum of Witchcraft (No. 1738)

55

In Suffolk, sea urchin fossils, locally called fairy loafs, are placed on the mantelpiece to magically ensure that there would always be bread in the house.

I remember collecting these as a child in Sussex where they are known as 'Shepherd's Crowns' and considered to be very lucky. In other regions they are called thunderstones. These beautiful fossils were placed amongst Neolithic and Bronze Age grave goods demonstrating that people have believed in their magical properties for thousands of years. The five pointed star marking of the sea urchin is of course an important occult symbol related to the pentagram.

Sea Urchin Fossils. Museum of Witchcraft (No. 834)

To Ensure a Good Harvest ❧
'Jump over a bonfire on Saint John's Eve' (the Summer Solstice).[8]

This is yet another ancient tradition that continued until comparatively recent times. It is quite possible that it originated as a pre-Christian purification ritual. Around the world, bonfires are still lit as part of Midsummer festivals.

To prevent accidents: *'First offer a sacrifice of bread and wine. Then gather selago whilst dressed in white with bare feet. The plant must be harvested with your right hand passed through the left sleeve of your tunic, as though committing a theft. Iron must not be used. Carry the selago with you.'* [9]

This old charm has several interesting 'ingredients' and raises several questions. To whom is this sacrifice made? Christ, a saint, God, a pre-Christian God? Why pass your right hand through your left sleeve? Could this be connected to the tradition of wearing your coat back to front or inside

8. Cielo, Astra. *Signs Omens and Superstitions,* 1918

9. *The Book of Witches,* 1908, p. 285

out to break a fairy spell? This theory is partly backed up by the spell forbidding the use of iron. In tradition, iron is said to protect you from fairies. Pliny confirms that selago (the herb of grace) must be cut without using iron. Harvesting 'as though committing a theft' may be related to other spells that use stolen meat, or possibly this is part of the spellcraft tradition of breaking away from the norm like writing prayers backwards.

When you have collected your magical selago, you might want to consider using this charm whilst making the bag to store it in:

This bag I sew for luck for me,
And also for my family
That it may keep by night and day
Trouble and illness far away.[10]

Luck for a Bridesmaid ✄

To ensure good luck, throw away a pin on the wedding day'.[11] And for the bride,

---

10. Huson, Paul. *Mastering Herbalism*
11. Cielo, Astra. *Signs Omens and Superstitions,* 1918

make sure that on her wedding day she
wears:

Something old
Something new
Something borrowed
Something blue.

In some versions a last line is added:

And a silver sixpence in her shoe.[12]

To Ensure Prosperity ❧
Carry a crust of bread in your pocket'.[13]

To Charm a Journey ❧

May the hills lie low,
May the sloughs fill up
In thy way.
May all evil sleep,
May all good awake,
In thy way.[14]

---

12. The Museum of Witchcraft Library & Archives
13. Cielo, Astra. *Signs Omens and Superstitions,* 1918
14. Macleod, Kenneth. *The Road to The Isles,* 1927

If not completely satisfied with this poetic old charm, maybe you should consider putting a protection amulet in your vehicle. Until recently, many cars would have a Saint Christopher medal dangling from the rear view mirror, and in Italy large, red replicas of the ancient mano cornuta (the horned hand), or cornicello (little horn) still hang amongst a plethora of protection amulets needed to make a safe journey. Having recently travelled in Italy, I can personally vouch for the necessity to carry multiple protection charms on any road journey.

A Protected Night's Sleep ⚜

Matthew, Mark, Luke, and John,
Bless the bed that I lie on;
There are four corners to my bed,
And four angles overspread,
Two at the feet, two at the head.
If any ill thing be betide,
Beneath your wings my body hide.
Matthew, Mark, Luke, and John
Bless the bed that I lie on. Amen.[15]

---

15. Heywood, John. *Lancashire Folk-lore,* 1882

There are many variants of this popular charm. The first verse above is also mentioned in *'A Candle in the Dark'*, a treatise on witchcraft by Thomas Ady in 1656 and in George Sinclair's *'Satan's Invisible World Discovered'* in 1685. It is sometimes known as the *'Black Paternoster'*. Although this charm is extremely old, it is still in use today and often considered to be a children's nursery rhyme.

It is interesting to compare the use of the 'four corners to my bed' with rituals used by older magical orders, such as 'The Golden Dawn' that include an invocation of the Archangels at each of the four cardinal points. Many modern wiccan rituals, drawing on traditional sources, start with 'calling the quarters' or 'watchtowers' in which symbolic guardians are called upon from each of the four quarters and asked to watch over the ritual.

In Ireland midwives would mark each outside corner of the house they were visiting with a cross and before entering repeat:

There are four corners to her bed,
Four angels at her head:
Matthew, Mark, Luke, and John,
God bless the bed that she lies on.
New Moon, New Moon, God bless me
God bless this house and family.[16]

This longer version was recorded in Suffolk. The collector of the charm notes that a 'ludicrous' variation to the forth line is sometimes used but does not explain what it is:

Matthew, Mark, Luke, and John,
Bless the bed that I lie upon;
Four corners to my bed,
And four angels at its head,
One to watch, two to pray,
And one to bear my soul away,
God within and God without,
Sweet Jesus Christ all round about
If I die before I wake,
I pray God my soul to take.[17]

---

16. from Rev. James Dugan M.A., T.C.D.
Heywood, John. *Lancashire Folk-lore*, 1882
17. Glyde, John. *The New Suffolk Garland*, 1866

I was recently amused to find a variant of the charm in use by an American Soft Ball team:

Matthew, Mark, Luke and John,
Bless this field we play upon.
Help us play with zeal and zest,
Help us play our very best.

Protection from (Bad) Witchcraft ✠

Hartland and Wilkinson tell us in their *'Folklore of Lancashire'* that: *'...according to a manuscript in Chetham's Library Manchester, Mother Bumby doth affirm...* [that] *the herb pimpernel is good to prevent witchcraft.' The following lines must be used when it is gathered;*

'Herb pimpernel I have found
Growing upon Christ Jesus' ground;
The same gift the Lord Jesus gave unto thee,
When He shed his blood upon the tree.
Arise up, pimpernel and go with me,
And God bless me,
And all that shall wear thee.
Amen.

Say this fifteen days together, twice a day; morning early fasting, and in the evening full.'

There is a reference to Mother Bumby in the play *'The Witch of Edmonton'* written in 1621.

Another more popular protection from curses is to make an equal armed cross of rowan wood, tied with red thread, and place it on a threshold door. There are many variants of this spell or charm, especially in Scotland where rowan wood and red thread are some of the most common ingredients in protection magic. Rowan berries are sometimes strung on red thread and worn as an amulet in the form of a necklace.[18]

George Sinclair wrote in 1685 *'...cut the Rouan-Tree between the two Beltan* [Beltane] *days. If any Man or Woman, Horse or Cow shall have a piece thereof upon them, no Devils or Fairy shall have the power to medle with them'.*[19]

The old folk song *'The Laidley Worm'* illustrates the power of rowan wood:

---

18. McNeill, F. Marian. *The Silver Bough*, 1956
19. Sinclair, George. *Satan's Invisible World Discovered*, 1685

... The spells were in vain; the hag returns
To the Queen in sorrowful mood
Crying that witches have no power
Where there is rowan-tree wood! [20]

It is said you can protect your home from witchcraft by simply planting a rowan tree adjacent to your front door. Or, to be even more secure, you could grow the tree over the portal to be protected: *'I have seen a rowan tree trained in the form of an arch over the byre door and in another case over the gate of the farm yard...'* wrote Dr James Napier in 1860.[21]

In northern Scotland, a branch of the rowan was placed over farmhouse doors, after having been waved while the words 'Avaunt, Satan!' were solemnly pronounced.[22]

Rowan tree and red thread feature in the ancient Scottish rhyme that lists amulets to ward off warlocks:

---

20. The Museum of Witchcraft Library & Archives
21. McNeill, F. Marian. *The Silver Bough*, 1956
22. Lawrence, Robert. *The Magic Of The Horse-Shoe,* 1889

Black-luggie, hammer-head,
Rowan tree and red thread,
Put the warlocks to their speed.[23]

In some versions of the rhyme, the second ingredient is lammer bead, possibly corrupted from 'amber bead', amber being another protection amulet favoured by witches. It has been suggested that 'black-luggie' might refer to blackthorn. Blackthorn is the wood used for making 'blasting rods', the wand that a witch traditionally would use to direct a curse.

Another version of this rhyme is:

Rowan, ash, and red thread,
Keep the devils frae their speed.[24]

And to protect cattle from witchcraft: *bind into the cow's tail a small piece of mountain-ash (rowan).*[25]

In Cornwall, the countryman that suspects one of his cattle has been

23. The Museum of Witchcraft Library & Archives
24. Thiselton Dyer, T.F. *English Folklore,* 1880
25. Brant, John. *Observations on Popular Antiquities,* 1842

overlooked (by the evil eye) *…runs to the nearest woods and brings home bunches of care* [rowan]*, which he suspends over the* [affected animal's] *stall, and wreathes round her horns.*[26]

Or in Lancashire: '*…cattle must be protected from witchery by sprogs of wiggen* [rowan] *over or in the shippens* [cowsheds]*.*'[27]

We can see that rowan wood is credited with special protection properties that reoccur time and time again, especially when used in conjunction with red thread. Indeed, simply carrying a piece of rowan wood secreted about you is said to be one of the best amulets to protect you from a witch's curse.

We have seen that by far the best known protection charm for cattle is attaching rowan to the creature, or to the beams of the cow shed, but there are other methods: '*Hang the first shoe put on the foot of a stallion, on the byre door, no harm will come near the cows.*'[28] Or, a spray or leaf of a four-leaf clover fixed

26. *Notes and Queries*, 1880

27. Heywood, John. *Lancashire Folk-lore*, 1882

28. Lawrence, Robert. *The Magic Of The Horse-Shoe*, 1889

to a cow should also do the trick.[29]

If a shrewmouse has run over one of your cattle, or if it has been exposed to a glance of the evil eye: *'gently stroke the affected animal with a twig from a "charmed" ash tree.'* We are told that an ash tree can be charmed by burying a horseshoe under it.[30]

To protect your house, tie a hag stone (a naturally holed stone) to your door key.[31] A variant of this charm is to tie a hag stone, or string of hag stones to the inside of your front and back doors. Odd numbers of stones are always used in a string.

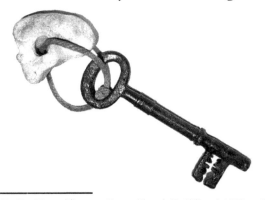

29. Davidson, Thomas. *Rowan Tree & Red Thread*, 1949, p. 59
30. Lawrence, Robert. *The Magic Of The Horse-Shoe*, 1889
31. The Museum of Witchcraft Library & Archives

There is a belief that circles confuse evil spirits, and that they cannot pass through them. This may account for the tradition of hag stones and of passing children and ill people through holed stones like the Mên-an-Tol in Cornwall – the person can pass through but the evil spirits are left behind.

Witch Bottles Against Curses ❧

For Thamson Leverton on Saterday next being the 17th of this Instant September any time that day take about a pint of your owne urine and make it almost scalding hot then Emtie it into a stone Jugg with a Narrow

Mouth then put into it so much white salt as you can take up with the Thumb and two forefingers of your lift hand and three new nails with their points downwards their points being first made very sharp then stop the mouth of the Jugg very close with a piece of Tough Cley and bind a piece of Leather firm over the stop then put the Jugg into warm embers and keep him there 9 or 10 days and nights following so that it go not stark cold all that meantime day nor night and your private Enemies will Never after have any power upon you either in Body or Goods so be it'.[32]

This instruction dates from the late 18th century, and describes a method of making a witch bottle to protect you from curses. Later in this book, we discuss the use of these devices to return a curse and harm the wrongdoer. This particular document is also important evidence that some charmers were educated and gave precise written instruction to their customers.

---

32. Cornwall Record Office, reference: X268/83

Cats to Protect Your House ✄

Amongst the other strange protection devices found in British cottages are cats that have been hidden in walls, under floors or in roofs. Many cats found in old buildings have simply crawled into a void and died. Some however (hundreds have been recorded) have clearly been deliberately and carefully placed in these locations for magical purposes. After death, these cats have been placed in position and occasionally they have dried out – sometimes preserving them for hundreds of years.

This cat has deliberately been set ready to pounce on a rat before being interred. Museum of Witchcraft (No. 1494)

A clue to their magical role may be that they are often deliberately set in a pouncing posture, sometimes with a mouse or rat close by. In life, a main role of the cat was to rid the house of unwanted vermin – could it be that after death the household cat was expected to carry on this duty and rid the house of spiritual vermin?

Ritual Marks – Witch Marks

Sometimes magical protection amulets are carved into the fabric of buildings; these are not the marks placed by carpenters or house builders to aid construction, but genuine magical sigils.

'Daisy Wheel' & 'Marion Marks' – Gemma Gary

Two styles are particularly prevalent in Britain; the 'daisy wheel' and the so-called Virgin Mary marks. These marks have been found on timbers and carved into stone, usually close to building thresholds and fireplaces. The 'daisy wheel' marks are clearly drawn with the aid of a pair of compasses and can have various numbers of petals, although six – the hex mark – is the most common. It is thought that they may have represented the sun which is often associated with good fortune.

The Virgin Mary or Marion mark consists of two 'V's overlapping, which can easily be mistaken for a 'W' or an 'M'. These marks may, as their name implies, be sigils associated with the Virgin Mary or *Virgo Virginum* – the Virgin of Virgins. Marks of this type have recently been found under the floor boards of a bedroom in the stately home of Knole in Kent. These marks have been dated to around 1606, so may well have been placed to protect King James I from witchcraft before his proposed visit to the house after the gun powder plot.

The areas around these marks sometimes show evidence of deliberate burning. This may indicate the marks were part of a charm against fire, in the belief that a timber burnt in this ritualised manner cannot catch fire again.

I find it fascinating that a large number of these 'Marion' marks have also been found at the entrance to Goatchurch Cavern in Somerset. The caves in this area have a long association with witchcraft, in particular The Witch of Wookey. Could it be that the scribe who placed these marks was calling on the power of the Virgin Mary to overcome the evil that was thought to lurk within the caves?

Shoes ≈

By far the most common magical object found secreted in old cottages is a single, old, worn shoe. These shoes are usually found on a ledge up a chimney, hidden in a wall, below floors or even in the thatch of a cottage. A shoe will hold an impression of its wearer's foot and that may be the reason it is such a common amulet. Elsewhere (see pages 199 & 200) in this book you will find charms that involve capturing the footprint of a person or animal, and these may well be related. Whoever placed the shoe in the building may have wanted the essence or spirit of its owner to remain, protecting and enchanting the building. It is interesting however that a lot of children's shoes have been found hidden in cottages; possibly this is related to the association of shoes with fertility. An old boot is often tied to the back of a wedding car, and a glance at a modern charm bracelet will confirm that it remains a popular good luck token.

Thanks are due to the extensive research made into folk magic and ritual archaeology by Brian Hoggard and Timothy Easton.

To Protect your House at Night ❧

Who sains the house the night,
They that sains it ilka night.
Saint Bryde and her brate,
Saint Colme and his hat,
Saint Michael and his spear,
Keep this house from the weir;
From running thief,

And burning thief;
And from and ill Rea,
That be the gate can gae;
And from an ill weight,
That be the gate can light
Nine reeds about the house;
Keep it all the night,
What is that, what I see
So red, so bright, beyond the sea?
'Tis he was pierc'd through the hands,
Through the feet, through the throat,
Through the tongue;
Through the liver and the lung.
Well is them that well may
Fast on Good-friday.[33]

To Protect a Child from the 'Evil Eye' 🌿

In 1956 Florence McNeill describes how after 'the words' had been spoken, a red knotted 'healing thread' of three ply is tied around the child's neck. The knots were then used like beads in a rosary; a line of incantation being repeated as each knot was passed. One of the incantations has survived:

---

33. Sinclair, George. *Satan's Invisible World Discovered*, 1685

An eye covered thee,
A mouth spoke thee
A heart envied thee
A mind desired thee.

Four made thy cross
Man and wife
Youth and maid;
Three will I send to thwart them:
Father,
Son,
Spirit Holy.

I appeal to Mary
Aidful Mother of men;
I appeal to Bride,
Foster Mother of Christ omnipotent;
I appeal to Columba,
Apostle of shore and sea;
And I appeal to heaven,
To all saints and angels that be above:

If it be a man that has done thee harm,
With evil eye,
With evil wish,
With evil passion,
Mayst thou cast off each ill,

Every malignity,
Every malice,
Every harassment,
And mayst thou be well for ever,
While this thread
Goes round thee,
In honour of God and of Jesus,
And of the Spirit of balm everlasting.[34]

To Protect a Boat from being 'Wiched' ✄

We have already spoken of the horseshoe being used to protect boats and ships, but we are also told to 'Nail or tie a holy stone in the bows, close beneath the gunwale'.[35]

A 'holy stone' (one with a natural hole in it) is another name for a hag stone, it rates amongst the most popular house and boat protection charms in Britian. In his 1906 article, Dr Colley March explains that in Abbotsbury, the rope used to haul the boats ashore is stowed by wrapping it around the sternpost and that the end of the rope is '...*threaded through a beach-*

---

34. McNeill, F. Marian. *The Silver Bough*, 1956. Also Carmicheal, Alexander. *Carminia Gadelica*, 1900
35. *Somerset & Dorset Notes & Queries*, Vol 10, 1906

holed-stone…' He further explains that this is to *'…keep any evil spirit, whether under the direction of a witch or not, from getting aboard the boat'*.

Written Charms ✒

Written charms are sometimes found hidden in buildings or placed in bottles. If you have made crosses of rowan wood, tied with red thread, and fixed them to the thresholds next to your horseshoes and hag stones but still feel the need for even more protection for your abode, you could follow the example of the Lancastrian charmer who wrote this charm and attached it over the door of a house in Burnley:

> *Sun, Moon, Mars, Mercury, Jupiter, Venus, Saturn, Trine, Sextile, Dragon's head, Dragon's tail, I charge you to guard this hause from all evils whatever, and guard it from all Desorders, and from aney thing being taken wrangasly, and give this family good Ealth & Welth.*[36]

---

36. Heywood, John. *Lancashire Folk-lore*, 1882

The advantage of a written charm is that it can be specifically tailored to a place, person or animal. For example this charm found at Devil's Bridge, Cardiganshire, in 1926 calls upon Christ to *'...relive Richard Davies and Gwarnas his mare that is bad now from all witchcraft and all evil diseases'.*[37]

We know that this charm will have been prepared for Mr Davies by a cunning man or woman because other similar examples exist in the same hand. This one, as is typical, incorporates writings

---

37. *MS 5563C*, National Library of Wales. Photo with kind permission.

from the old Grimoires (books of magic) along with magical talismans.

Some of the text in this manuscript is from *'The Discoverie of Witchcraft'* (Reginald Scot, 1584) as is the talisman. The use of the ancient abracadabra triangle is also very common in this type of written magic. But perhaps the most fascinating observation relating to this charm is that it dates from around the time of the First World War – the creator of this document was at the end of an unbroken line of magical practitioners dating back hundreds of years. The charm, made for Richard Davis in the early 1900s, would have been recognised and understood by occultists of the 16th century.

In the name of the Father and of the son and the Holy ghost amen xxx and in the name of the Lord Jesus Christ his redeemer and saviour he will relieve Richard Davies and Gwarnas his mare that is bad now from all witchcraft and all evil diseases amen xxx Gasper fert myrrham Thus melchior balthasar aurum hoec tria qui sequm salvatur amorbo a Christ pietate caduco amen xxx ineducto un iversanilam ama thuram deapt positis sarah adversus artedovalis amen xxx *eructavit cor meaum verbum bonum dicam cuncta opera mea regi domine labia mea aperies and os meum annuntiabit veritatem contre bracnia iniquet rei lingua melinqua subertatur a Lord Jesus Christ hommaum aluctus he hereth the preserver of Richard Davies Gwarnas his mare that is bad now from all witchcraft and evill men or women or spirits or wizards or hardness of hart amen* xxx *and this I will trust in the Lord Jesus Christ thy redeemer and saviour from witchcraft amen* xxx *and this I trust in Jesus Christ thy redeemer and saviour he will relieve Richard Davies his mare that is bad now from all witchcraft by the same power as he did cause the blind to see the lame to walk and the dum to talk and that thou findest with unclean spirits as wilt Jehovah amen* xxx *The witch compased them about but the Lord will destroy them all pater pater pater noster noster noster ave ave ave maria creed car of acteum* x *on* x *adona* x *Tetragrammaton amen* xxx *and in the name of the Holy Trinity and of* [their] *number it preserve all above named from all evil diseases whatsoever amen* x

82

Pincushion Charm
The Museum of Witchcraft (No. 1211)

Spells, Charms & Divinations
for Love

I t seems that people's desire to fall
in love, or at least know if, when,
and who they will fall in love with,
has kept the spell and charm makers
busy. Every region of the British
Isles has its own variant of the many
predictive chants that will forecast what
type of person you will marry or fall in
love with.

*Tinker, tailor, soldier, sailor, rich man, poor
man, beggar man, thief.*

Many say that it is unwise to cast love
spells or concoct love potions; after all
you could be forcing someone to love

you (or another) against his or her will. This ethical dilemma does not seem to have deterred the wise woman or man of old, as is evident by the quantity of these charms and regularity at which they occur.

Below are listed a selection of spells and charms to make somebody love you, or ro regain a lover.

To Cause Love or Regain a Lover

Buy three pennyworth of dragon's blood. Don't eat or drink between eleven and twelve at night; as the clock strikes twelve place the dragon's blood on a piece of white paper in the grate and set it alight. While burning keep the name of your lover in mind and repeat the following:

Dragon's blood, dragon's blood.
Tis not your blood I wish to burn
But my true love's heart I wish to turn.
May he never sleep, rest nor happy be,
Until he comes or send to me.[38]

38. Semmens, Jason. *The Cornish Witch Finder,* p.178

Postcard c 1910 from The Museum of Witchcraft collection

This charm was one of the many collected by the Cornish folklorist William Paynter in the early 1900s. I am indebted to Jason Semmens for making them available to us in his book *The Cornish Witch-finder*. Another version of this charm is:

> *'Tis not this blood I mean to burn,*
> *But my love's heart I wish to turn.*
> *May he no pleasure see*
> *Until that he comes back to me.'* [39]

A.R. Wright in his leaflet *'English Folklore'* suggests that *'there are still (in 1928) girls in London and in many country districts who throw dragon's blood into the fire to regain a false lover, or burn tormentil root (potentilla tormentilla) at midnight on a Friday for the same purpose.'*

I should explain that dragon's blood is a bright red resin (calamus draco) that is obtained from various plants and that no dragons need be harmed whilst carrying out this spell! And yet

---

39. Wright, R.A. *English Folklore*, 1928

another version uses salt, ...*throwing a little salt into the fire on three successive Friday nights, while saying these words:*

'It is not this salt I wish to burn,
It is my lover's heart to turn;
That he may neither rest nor happy be,
Until he comes and speaks to me.' [40]

On St John's Day, place a frog in a pot that has small holes in it and place it in an anthill. After the ants have reduced the frog to a skeleton, grind it with bat's blood and dried powdered flies. Shape into pellets and add to the food of the person whose love you desire. [41]

A variant of this charm can be found in a copy of an old manuscript in the Museum of Witchcraft Archive:

Take a frog... and put him into a pot, that is made full of holes and stop it fast and bury the pot in a cross highway in an ant hill... and let

---

40. Lawrence, Robert. *The Magic Of The Horse-Shoe,* 1889
41. *Magical Charms Potions & Secrets for Love,* 1972

*it be there nine days… and at the nine days' end
go and take out the pot and thou shalt find two
bones in it, take them and put them in a running
water, and one of them will float against the
stream…. And make thee a ring and take thee
of it that swum against the stream, and put it
in the ring, and when you will have any woman
and put it on her right hand.*[42]

Plant a flower bulb in a clean clay
pot that has never been used before.
Repeat a beloved's name thrice and
then chant:

*As this root grows
And as its blossom blows
May my true love's heart be,
Softly turned unto me.*[43]

The wise-woman must go on
their left knee and pluck nine roots
of pearlwort. These she must knot
together to form a ring which must be

42. Copy of 16th/17th century manuscript of
magician's notes in The Museum of Witchcraft archive
43. Pepper, Elizabeth. *Magic Spells & Incantations,* 2001

placed in the mouth of the girl who
sought aid saying:

*'In he name of King of the sun, the moon,
and the stars, and in the name of the Holy
Three.'*
    *The girl must persuade the man she desires
to kiss her whilst the ring is in her mouth
and he will become her bondman.*[44]

When plucking the pearlwort the
charmer might well have used this charm:

*I will cull the pearwort
Beneath the fair sun of Sunday
Beneath the hand of the Virgin,
In the name of the Trinity
Who willed it to grow.*

*While I shall keep the pearlwort
Without ill mine eye
Without harm my mouth
Without grief my heart
Without guile my death.*[45]

---

44. McNeill, F. Marian. *The Silver Bough*, 1956
45. *Ibid*

Postcard c 1910 from The Museum of Witchcraft collection

This spell is from 1723:

...he threads a needle with the hair of her head, and then running it through the fleshy part of a dead man, as the brawn of the arms, thigh, or the calf of the leg, the charm has virtue in it, as to make her run mad for him...[46]

Obtain the bones of a green frog, which has been eaten inside an ant-heap. Throw the bones into water; one part floats above the water and the other sinks to the bottom. Wrap the floating bones in silk and hang them around your neck,

---

46. Brant, John. *Observations on Popular Antiquities*, 1842

and you will be loved. If you touch a man
with them hate will come of it.[47]

To Fall Out of Love

A Charm or an Allay for love, from
Herrick's *Hesperides* written in the 1640s:

> *If so be a Toad be laid*
> *In a sheep-skin newly flaid*
> *And that ty'd to man, 'twill sever*
> *Him and his affections ever.* [48]

If You Wish to Marry

The couple must take the church key and
place it over the sixth and seventh verses of
the eighth chapter of the Song of Solomon:

> *Set me a seal upon thine heart, as a seal upon*
> *thine arm; for love is strong as death; jealousy is*
> *cruel as the grave; the coals thereof are coals of*
> *fire, which hath a most vehement flame. Many*
> *waters cannot quench love, neither can the floods*
> *drown it; if a man would give all the substance of*
> *his house for love, it would utterly be contemned.*

---

47. *The Book of Witches*, 1908
48. Brant, John. *Observations on Popular Antiquities*, 1842

Over the words they must hold the church key, balancing it by the end; and if the wards of the key incline towards the verses, which by skilful manipulation they can easily be made to do, it is a sign that the course of true love will run smooth.[49]

To Make a Woman Answer Truly ❧

In 1533 the occult writer, researcher and collector Heinrich Cornelius Agrippa quoted the Ancient Greek philosopher Democritus:

If any one take out the tongue of a water-frog, yet living, no other part of the body sticking to it, and it be let go into the water again, and lay it [the tongue] *upon the place where a woman's heart beats, she shall answer truly whatsoever you ask her.*

To Keep a Man in Love with His Wife ❧

If a wife will hold her husband to her in love, she must take of her own hair and bind it to his. This must be done three times by full moonlight.[50]

---

49. Glyde Junior, John. *The New Suffolk Garland,* 1866
50. *The Book of Charms and Ceremonies,* 1910

Ingredients to Cause Love or Hatred ❧

Take all the young swallows from one nest; put them into a pot and bury them until they die from hunger. Those that have died with their beaks open will excite love, and those with their beaks closed will bring hatred.[51]

It is thought that the dead swallows were placed under the bed or pillow of the person into whom love would 'be excited'.

Dead Swift Charm, Museum of Witchcraft (No. 1019)

To Make a Woman Return Your Love ❧

On Friday early as may be,
Take the fairest apple from a tree,
Then in thy blood on paper white,
Thy own name and thy true loves write,
That apple thou in two shalt cut
And for its cure that paper put,
With two sharp pins of myrtle wood,

---

51. *The Book of Witches*, 1908, p.291

In the oven let it dry,
And wrapped in leaves of myrtle lie,
Under the pillow of thy dear,
Yet let it be unknown to her;
And if it a secret be
She soon will show her love for thee.[52]

To Know the Type of Man You'll Marry

Take a walnut, a hazel nut, a nutmeg; grate them together and mix them with butter and sugar, and make them into small pills. Take nine pills on going to bed and your dreams will show the state of the person you will marry:

riches – a gentleman, white linen – a clergyman, darkness – a lawyer, noises and tumults – a tradesman, thunder & lightning – a soldier or sailor, rain – a servant. [53]

To Know Your Future Husband's Trade

Get a glass of water, and having broken an egg, and separated the white from the yoke, throw the former into it, and place it in the sunshine. You will soon see, with

---

52. *The Book of Charms and Ceremonies*, 1910
53. *Ibid*, p.7

a little aid from your fancy, the ropes and yards of a vessel, if your husband is to be a sailor, or plough and team, if he is to be a farmer.[54]

To Test a Prospective Wife

Ascertain what day of the month the ladies birthday falls. Compare this day with the corresponding verse from the thirty-one verses in the last chapter of the Book of Proverbs. You will thus find out what kind of life you will lead with her in the event of marriage.

The collector of this charm also points out that this will give you the opportunity to opt out of marrying someone unsuitable! [55]

To Enchant a Maiden into Furious Love

The hair from the belly of a goat, tied into knots, and concealed in the roof of the house of the beloved, will produce furious love, whereby the maiden will not be able to withstand

54. Couch, Jonathan. *The History of Polrerrow*, 1871
55. Glyde Junior, John. *The New Suffolk Garland*, 1866

the entreaties of her lover, but will be so enchanted with him that marriage will soon take place.[56]

To Make a Love Potion 🌿

There is a little venomous piece of flesh as big as a fig, and black, which is in the forehead of a colt newly foaled, called Hippomanes. If it be powdered and mixed with the blood of him that is in love it hath a most powerful philter to cause love.[57]

This spell is also found in *'The Book of Charms and Ceremonies'* by 'Merlin' published in 1910.

I find it fascinating and intriguing that such a peculiar spell should be selected for inclusion in Merlin's book some 380 years after its original publication. I am however pleased to continue the tradition by reprinting it here, now over 470 years since Agrippa scribed it!

---

56. Attrib Agrippa *The Book of Charms & Ceremonies*, 1910
57. Agrippa, 1533

To Win the Love of a Maid

Get some willow knots, cut one of them and put it into your mouth, and say:

I eat thy luck,
I drink thy luck,
Give me that luck of thine,
Then thou shalt be mine.

Then if thou canst, hide the knot in the bed of the wished-for bride.[58]

To Bring Back an Absent Lover

To bring back an absent lover, a woman must gather an oak twig with an attached acorn cup and also some ash twigs. These must be put under her pillow for three nights. Each night, on retiring, she must say:

Bid my true love come to me.
Between moonlight and firelight,
Bring him over the hill tonight,
Over the meadows, over the moor,
Over the rivers and over the sea,

---

58. *The Book of Charms and Ceremonies*, 1910

Over the threshold and in at the door
Acorn cup and ashen key,
Bring my true love back to me.[59]

Spells to See Your Future Husband ✄

Go to a crossroads on St George's
night and comb your hair backwards.
Prick the little finger of your left hand
and let three drops of blood fall to the
ground whilst saying:

I give my blood to my loved one.
Whom I shall see shall be mine own.

The form of your future husband
will rise out of the blood and slowly
fade away. Gather the dust or blood
mud and throw it into a river or you
will be drowned within the year.[60]

It would be wise to concentrate whilst
performing this spell; the consequences
of forgetting to dispose of the ingredients
properly are rather severe! Tradition has
it that one should concentrate hard on

59. The Museum of Witchcraft Library & Archives
60. Leyland, Charles. *Gypsy Sorcery & Fortune Telling*, 1891

any spell or charm; the more effort put in the better the results.

Unmarried women, on going to bed, should place their shoes at right angles in the form of the letter T, thrice repeating the following lines:

Hoping this night my husband to see,
I place my shoes in the form of a T,
Trusting he'll come with features quite fair,
My waiting heart to free from great care.[61]

Let three young women join in making a chain a yard long, of Christmas juniper and mistletoe berries, and at the end of each link put an oak acorn. Exactly before midnight let them assemble in a room by themselves. Leave a window open and take the key out of the keyhole and hang it over the chimney-piece. Have a good fire and place in the midst of it a long, thinnish, log of wood well-sprinkled with salt, oil, and fresh mould. Then wrap the chain round it, each maiden having an equal share of the business. Then sit

61. *The Book of Charms & Ceremonies*, 1910, p.29

down, and, on your left knee, let each
fair one have a prayer book opened at
the matrimonial service. Just as the last
acorn is burst the future husband will
cross the room. Each will see her own
proper spouse, but he will be invisible
to the rest of the wakeful virgins. Those
that are not to wed will see a coffin or
some misshapen form cross the room.

Go to bed and you will have remarkable
dreams. This must be done only on a
Wednesday or Friday night.[62]

Get nine small keys of your own
(borrowing will not do, nor must you tell
what you want them for). Plait a three-
plaited band of your own hair, and tie
them together, fastening the ends with
nine knots; fasten them with one of
your garters to your left wrist on going
to bed, and bind the other garter round
your head, then say:

St Peter, take it not amiss,
To try your favour I've done this;
You are the ruler of the keys,

62. *The Book of Charms & Ceremonies*, 1910, p.27

Favour me then, if you please;
Let me then your influence prove;
And see my dear and wedded love.[63]

Notice that nine knots are used in the hair plait – similar to *'the nine witch knots braided in amongst my ladies locks'* in the old ballad *Willie's Lady* (see pages 226-231). In the ballad the knots are a spell against childbirth. The nine knots form a 'witch's ladder' (see page 135).

Rise between three and four o'clock on your birthday, and go secretly and silently into the garden, pluck a sprig of laurel, take it to your room, and hold it for five minutes over some lighted brimstone. Note the time then wrap the laurel in a fair white linen cloth together with a paper on which is written your name and the name of your lover, or, if you have many suitors, each name, the day of the week, the date of the year, and the age of the moon also being inscribed. Then quickly go and bury the packet in the ground. It must

---

63. *Ibid,* p. 27/28

not be disturbed for three days and three nights, but you may then take it up. Place it under your pillow for three nights, when you will certainly dream of the man who will lead you to the altar.[64]

To See Your Future Lover

On finding yarrow growing on the grave of a man who had died young, recite:

> *Yarrow, sweet Yarrow,*
> *The first that I have found,*
> *In the name of Jesus,*
> *I pluck you from the ground;*
> *As Joseph loved sweet Mary*
> *And took her for his dear,*
> *So in a dream this night*
> *I hope my true love will appear.*[65]

Other popular versions of this charm in modern circulation call on 'the Lady' or 'Horny' in place of Jesus.

It does seem rather odd to call on Jesus in this type of love charm, especially as

---

64. *Ibid,* p.30
65. *Gardeners Chronicle,* 1875

we are told that he remained a single man. Plucking plants from a dead man's grave also hints at an older, less delicate origin than the rhyme suggests.

Peel an onion, wrap it in a clean handkerchief and place this under your pillow saying:

Good St. Thomas, do me right,
And see my true love come to-night,
That I may see him in the face,
And him in my kind arms embrace.[66]

Get some hemp seed, take it into the garden at midnight and, scattering it, repeat the words:

Hemp seed I sow, hemp seed I hoe,
In hopes that my true love will come after me
and mow.

You will then see the apparition of your future lover with a scythe, in the act of mowing.[67]

---

66. Thiselton Dyer, T.F. *English Folklore*, 1880
67. Couch, Jonathan. *The History of Polrerrow*, 1871

Spread bread and cheese on the table and sit down to it alone, observing strict silence. As the clock strikes the hour of midnight, your future lover will join you at supper.[68]

Get a piece of wedding cake, and carry it upstairs backwards. Tie it in your left stocking, with your right garter, and place it under your pillow. Get into bed backwards, keeping strict silence all the while, and your dream will reveal to you your predestined sweetheart. These 'ceremonies due' must be done aright, or the divination fails.[69]

A clover or two, if you put in your shoe,
The next man you meet in field or lane
Will be your husband, or one of the name.

The collector of this charm said that it was still in use (1866) by the maidens of Suffolk.[70]

---

68. *Ibid*

69. Couch, Jonathan. *The History of Polrerrow*, 1871

70. Glyde Junior, John. *The New Suffolk Garland*, 1866

To Cause Your Wife to be Faithful ✄

....*a young graft being thrust through a Frogs guts, and fastened by the Husband in his Wife's flowers, then will cause his Wife to loath adultery.*[71]

To Know if a Pretended Lover is True ✄

....the maiden takes an apple pip, and naming one of her followers, puts the pip in the fire. If it makes a noise in bursting, from the heat, it is proof of love; but if it is consumed without a crack, she is fully satisfied that there is no real regard towards her...[72]

---

71. Bromhall, Thomas. *A Treaties of Specters*, 1658
72. Glyde Junior, John. *The New Suffolk Garland*, 1866

Healing Charms

Wishing You Well

Not many generations ago, across most of Britain, the first port-of-call when a family member was seriously unwell was often the local charmer; the wise woman or cunning man. Whilst many of the remedies offered by these healers were straight-forward medicines, a good percentage contained elements of magic. In compiling this chapter, I have avoided cures unless they contain a strong magical component. I am not including the astrological associations of plants, as to do so would simply replicate the wonderful old herbals like Culpepper's (first published in 1663), many of which are still in print today. In making this decision I am not ignoring the magic of herbal remedies –

I well remember being stung by nettles as a child and the instant relief granted by the application of dock leaves:

Nettle in, Dock out,
Dock in, Nettle out,
Nettle in, Dock out,
Dock rub, Nettle out.[73]

The antiquity, popularity, and resilience of some of these old remedies can be demonstrated by taking a look at the 'Bone to Bone' charm which is over 900 years old and still going strong:

Bone to bone,
And vein to vein
And vein turn to thy rest again.
And so shall thine [the name of the injured person].[74]

This charm has been translated, transformed, reduced, and expanded many times but still retains the poetic and

---

73. *The Book of Witches*, 1908, p. 286
74. *Devon & Cornwall Notes & Queries*, 1911

magical quality that is common to many of the best spells and charms – it remains recognisable and is regularly used by 21st century charmers.

The earliest known record of 'Bone to Bone' is from a document in Merseburg Cathedral Library in Germany. The charm is written in a 10th Century hand on a blank page of a 9th Century document, although the Pre-Christian nature of the incantation indicates that its origin is much older:

Phol ende uuodan uuorun zi holza.
du uuart demo balderes uolon sin uuoz birenkit.
thu biguol en sinthgunt, sunna era suister;
thu biguol en friia, uolla era suister;
thu biguol en uuodan, so he uuola conda:
sose benrenki, sose bluotrenki, sose lidirenki:
ben zi bena, bluot si bluoda,
lid zi geliden, sose gelimida sin!

Phol and Woden were riding in the woods.
And Balder's foal twisted its ankle.
Then Sindgun (and) Sunna, her sister,
chanted a spell over it:
Then Frija, Volla's sister, chanted a spell over it:

Then Woden chanted a spell over it as well he could:
Like the sprain of the bone,
So the sprain of the blood,
So the sprain of the limb.
Bone to bone, blood to blood,
Joint to joint, thus glued together be!

Clearly this charm was to cure a horse's sprained or twisted ankle, but over hundreds of years of use it has been used to cure many other aliments, notably broken bones:

This is the spell that I intone,
Flesh to flesh and bone to bone
Sinew to sinew and vein to vein
And each one shall be whole again.[75]

In Shetland, to cure a sprain it was customary to apply a 'wresting thread'. This is a thread spun from black wool, on which are cast nine knots and is tied round a sprained leg or arm. Whilst tying the thread, this charm is whispered so that the bystanders or the recipient cannot hear it;

75. The Museum of Witchcraft Library & Archives

The Lord rade,
And the foal slade;
He lighted.
And he righted.
Set joint to joint,
Bone to bone,
And sinew to sinew.
Heal in the Holy Ghost's Name! [76]

In Orkney, a similar charm was used for sprains with linen thread tied around the injured part. Nine knots would be tied at regular distances along the cord and the charm would be repeated for each knot:

Our Saviour rade,
His fore-foot slade;
Our Saviour lichtit down.
Sinew to sinew,
Vein to vein,
Joint to joint,
And bane to bane,
Mend thou in God's name! [77]

---

76. *The New Statistical Account of Scotland,* 1845, vol. 15
Shetland. Also McNeill, F. Marian. *The Silver Bough,* 1956
77. *Orkney Charms, Notes and Queries,* series 1, vol. 10

Note the tying of nine knots in a cord. This is similar to the 'witch's ladder' (described on page 135) and also reminds us of the *'nine witch knots'* that were *'braided in amongst my lady's locks'* in the folk ballad Willie's Lady (see pages 226-231).

It is apparent that the main difference between these charms from the Scottish Isles and the earlier German spell is the deity involved. In the later spells, the pre-Christian god Woden (sometimes known as Wodan or Odin) is replaced with 'The Lord' or 'Our Saviour' and the healing is completed in the name of 'God' or the 'Holy Ghost'. Over 900 or more years, the spell has become completely Christianised. One has to wonder if the Christian versions were more or less effective than the older, pagan form.

Notice that in some variants of the 'Bone to Bone' charm, Christ is riding across a bridge. This may be significant as there is a tradition that witches and spirits are unable to cross running water:

As Christ was riding over cross a bridge, his leg he took and blessed it, and said these words;

Bone to Bone
Sinnes to Sinnes
Vains to Vains
He blessed it, and it come hole again.
In the name of the Father, and of the Son,
and of the Holy Ghost.
Amen.[78]

From Dunstone in Devon:
As Christ was riding over Mercy Bridge,
His horse fell down and broke his leg
He uttered these words and said;
Bone to bone
Sane to sane [a corruption of vein to vein?]
Soon he was well and whole again
In the name of the Trinity.[79]

From Polperro in Cornwall:
Christ rode over the bridge,
Christ rode under the bridge;
Vein to vein
Strain to Strain,
I hope God will take it back againe.[80]

---

78. *Devonshire Association Folk-Lore Transactions,* 1862 -1928
79. *Ibid*
80. Couch, Jonathan. *The History of Polperro,* 1871

From Marystowe, Devon:

Our Lord Jesus Christ rode over a bridge.
His horse lighted and he lighted. He said
Marrow to Marrow,
And bone to bone
And sinews to sinews
And blood to blood
And skin to skin.
In the name of the Father, and of the Son, and
of the Holy Ghost, I cast this sprain away.
Amen. So be it.[81]

There are so many examples of the Bone to Bone charm that I could fill this book, so I will make this more unusual example from Shropshire my last:

Our Saviour Jesus Crist roate on a marbel Stone
Senow to Senow
Joint to Joint
Bone to Bone
He roat thes wordes everey one
In the name of the Father Sone and Holey Gost
Amen Swet Jesus
Amen Swet Jesus.
Amen.[82]

---

81. *Devonshire Association Folk-Lore Transactions*, 1862 -1928
82. *Folklore*, Vol. 6, No. 2, June 1895

To Reset Out of Joint Bones ✤
Use the charm: *'Danata, daries, dardaries, astataries.'* [83]

To Cure Illness ✤
Write *Hax, pax, max, Deus adimax* on an apple and give it to the patient to eat.[84]

If an apple is cut in half across the main axis, a pentacle pattern is revealed by the pips. Nature has imbued the apples with a magical occult symbol that has encouraged their use in so many spells and charms.

To Cure the Bloody Flux ✤
To cure this and other illnesses, hang a Good Friday loaf in the corner of your cottage. Give the patient some of the loaf to eat. In *'The New Suffolk Garland'* printed in 1866, John Glyde tells us that *'...such loaves were far from uncommon in this parish.'* He also adds that *'loaves backed on Good Friday never get mouldy.'*

83. *The Book of Witches*, 1908, p. 282
84. *Ibid*

To Cure Inflammations

To cure ringworm, wild titters, burn-gout, itching gout, smarting gout, water-gout, chicken-pox, St Tanterous fire, girdleing etc:

> *There was three brothers*
> *come from the North West going to the South,*
> *to kill and to cure (name the person in full)*
> *for ringworm, wild titters,*
> *burn – gout, itching gout,*
> *smarting gout, water gout,*
> *chicken-pox, St Tanterous fire,*
> *girdleing or whatsoever it may be,*
> *in the name of the Father, Son, and Holy Ghost.*
> *Amen.*

In using this, the charmer hung a branch of whitethorn on a wall, without letting it touch the ground. Then she took nine small pieces of different coloured cloth tied in a bunch, and some raw cream. The patient sat under the thorn, the bits of cloth were dipped into the cream and 'dapped' upon the ringworm. It must be done 5, 7, 9, 11, 13, or any odd number of times before the charmer or patient had broken their fast.[85]

To cure Ague (Malaria or Fever) ❧
Take the invalid's hand and say:

'Acque facilis tibi febris haec fit, atque Mariae Virgini Christi partus.' [86]

Or, to cure yourself, write the following on a piece of paper and hang it around your neck: [87]

A B R A C A D A B R A
A B R A C A D A B R
A B R A C A D A B
A B R A C A D A
A B R A C A D
A B R A C A
A B R A C
A B R A
A B R
A B
A

85. *Devonshire Association Folk-Lore Transactions*, 1862 -1928
86. *The Book of Witches*, 1908
87. *Ibid*

This classic and ancient spell is diminishing the magical word ABRACADABRA line by line. In this example the full word is written on the top and it reduces to a single letter at the bottom.

This is sympathetic magic; as the word diminishes, so does the ailment. A spell for the patient to build up strength after an illness would involve an ABRACADABRA triangle with the single 'A' on top:

```
              A
            A B
          A B R
        A B R A
      A B R A C
    A B R A C A
  A B R A C A D
A B R A C A D A
A B R A C A D A B
A B R A C A D A B R
A B R A C A D A B R A
```

Another variant on this theme is given in *'The Book of Charms and Ceremonies'*, (1910):

'*If it were required to perform a cure at a distance... let the charm* [abracadabra] *be written on virgin parchment* [parchment that has not been used before]... *Scrape out one line of the charm every day with a new knife, kept express for the purpose; and at scraping out each line, say as follows:*

"*So as I destroy the letters of this charm, Abracadabra, so, by virtue of this sacred name, may all grief and dolour depart from A.*B. *[the name of the patient] in the name of the Father, and of the Son, and of the Holy Ghost. In the name of the Father I destroy this disease, In the name of the Son I destroy this disease, In the name of the Holy Spirit I destroy this disease.*

Amen.'

The anonymous author of the book adds that:

'*Many have healed divers diseases this way; the disease wearing, little and little, away. Therefore keep it secret, and fear God*'.

This charm was also recorded some 400 years earlier in a manuscript of magician's notes held by The Museum of Witchcraft.[88]

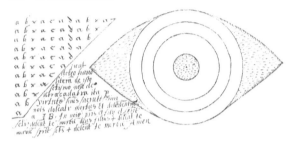

Church communion wafers have also been used to cure fever; take three holy wafers, and write on the first, 'So is the Father, so is life'; on the second, 'So is the Son, so is the Saint'; on the third, 'So is the Holy Ghost, so is the remedy'. Take the wafers to the fever patient and tell him to eat them on three consecutive days; neither eating nor drinking anything else; also say fifteen times daily the Pater and the Ave.[89]

---

88. Copy of 16th/17th century manuscript of magician's notes (once owned by Robert Lenkiewicz) held in The Museum of Witchcraft Archive
89. *The Book of Witches*, 1908, p.283

Communion wafers are thought to be more effective if they have been consecrated, and some spells direct the participant to attend a church mass and secrete the host rather than eating it.

Or, if you can't get hold of holy wafers, cut an apple in three, write on one piece *'Increatus Pater'*, on another *'Immensus Pater'*, and on the last *'Aeternus Pater'*. Let the patient eat them on three separate days whilst fasting.[90] Alternatively, place a spider or its web in a small piece of apple and swallow it.[91]

Oliver Maddox Hueffer in his *'The Book of Witches'* (1908) does not tell us where he found this old fever cure:

> *'For feaver wryt thys words on a lorell lef +*
> *Ysmael + Ysmael + adjuro vos per angelum*
> *ut soporetur iste Homo. And ley thys lef*
> *under hys head that he wete not thereod and let*
> *hym ete Letuse oft and drynk Ip'e seed small*
> *grounden in a mortar and temper yt with ale.'* [92]

---

90. *Ibid*

91. Glyde, John. *The New Suffolk Garland*, 1866

92. *The Book of Witches*, 1908

Translated into modern English:

*For fever write these words on a laurel leaf +
Ysmael + Ysmael + adjuro vos per angelum
ut soporetur iste Hom. Lye the leaf under
his head that has not been made wet* [with
sweat?] *and let him eat lettuce often and
drink Ip'e* [?] *seed ground small in a mortar
and temper it with ale.*

Hueffer suggests visiting *'a crossroads
five different times at the dead of night and
there bury a new laid egg... this has never been
known to fail'.* In the 1842 *'Observations
on Popular Antiquities'* the same charm is
attributed to a Mr. Douce's manuscript
which states that it is very popular with
persons about Exeter.[93]

Hueffer also draws our attention to the
English astrologer Elias Ashmole, who
in 1661 wrote:

*'I took early in the morning a good dose of
elixir and hung three spiders about my neck;
they drove my ague away.'*

---

93. *The Book of Witches,* 1908

This is another good example of 'passing-on magic' – as the spiders take on the illness and die, the fever also dies.[94]

To Cure Ague, Fever or Witchcraft

When Jesus saw the Cross, thare to be crucified, pilate said unto him "What aileth thee?" why shakes thou? Hast thou fever, ague or witchcraft?" Jesus said unto him "I have neither fever ague nor witchcraft, but shake for thy sins." Whosoever carryeth this in his mind or in writing shall never have neither fever, ague nor witchcraft – in the name of the father and of the Son and of the holy ghost. Amen and Amen.[95]

This unusual charm was discovered amongst papers in Marystow, Devon. Another variant of this charm is found in Polperro, Cornwall:

When our saviour saw the cross, whereon he was to be crucified, his body did shake. The

94. *Ibid*, p. 281
95. *Devonshire Association Folk-Lore Transactions*, 1862 -1928

Jews said, 'Hast thou an ague!' Our Saviour said, 'He that keepeth this in mind, thought, or writing, shall neither be troubled with ague or fever'.[96]

In the 1860s the Reverend Hugh Pigot of Hadleigh, Suffolk, whilst suffering from the ague, was urged to *'go to a stile – one of those placed across foot-paths – and to drive a nail into that part over which foot passengers travel in their journeys'.[97]* I suspect that this charm is intended to pass on the ague to the next person that trod on the style. I wonder if the Reverend realised that the nature of this charm was not very Christian.

The colour red, nail parings, a lock of hair, stolen meat, black cloth – so many classic ingredients are included in this fine old spell to cure fever that it is hard to believe that it could fail!

Purchase a new red earthen pan, into which place parings of your finger and

---

96. Couch, Jonathan. *The History of Polperro*, 1871
97. Glyde, John. *The New Suffolk Garland*, 1866

toe nails, together with a lock of hair and a small piece of stolen, raw, beef. Tie a piece of black silk over the pan and bury it in the centre of a wood in ground that has never before been broken. As the meat decays the fever will abate and finally disappear.[98]

In the 16th Century, Agrippa says that a cure for fever is to get a bone from the body of a dead man who never had the fever, and lay it upon the patient *'..when he will be cured of his malady'*. He also says that:

'Menstrual Blood drives away tertian, and quartane Agues, if it be put into the wool of a black Ram, and tied up in a silver bracelet, as also if the soles of the patients feet be anointed therewith, and especially if it be done by the woman herself, the patients not knowing of it; moreover it cures the fits of the falling sickness.'[99]

---

98. *Ibid*
99. Agrippa. Book 1 chap. Xlii

Alternatively, we are told that:

'the chips or cuttings of a gibbet, or gallows, on which one or more persons have been executed or exposed, if worn next to the skin or around the neck in a bag, will cure the Ague or prevent it.' [100]

To cure wens (a growth or cyst) a correspondent for *'The Times'* newspaper, reporting from the site of a public execution in 1819, writes:

'After the body had hung some time, several persons applied for permission to rub the hand of the deceased over their Wens... as a cure for those troublesome swellings'. [101]

A similar charm is recorded in Suffolk:

'Pass the hand of a dead body over the part affected, on three successive days'.

---

100. Brant, John. *Observations on Popular Antiquities*, 1842
101. *Ibid*

The collector of this charm in 1866 says that *The Rev. Hugh Pigot has known this to be tried at Hadleigh.*[102] If you are looking for other uses for your hanged man's hand see also (on pages 225-258) The Hand of Glory!

To Cure Hard Swellings ✒

'Take the hand of a person who has died an immature death, and gently rub the throat where the hard swelling or imposthume is situated, and it will disappear and trouble the patient no more'.[103]

The anonymous author of the book of charms in which I found this cure does not say how one acquires the hand of the dead person, but in the days of public executions, the hands of executed convicts were highly valued for their magical properties. It is also reported that the hand of a dead shipwrecked sailor from the S.S. Uppingham (wrecked in 1890) was used by villagers for 'striking the king's evil'.[104]

102. Glyde, John. *The New Suffolk Garland,* 1866

103. *The Book of Charms and Ceremonies,* 1910

104. *Devonshire Association Folk-Lore Transactions,* 1906

A reference is also made to a dead man's hand curing a terrible tumour in 1888, apparently the method was to '...*take the hand, cross it nine times over the wound, and then, as the hand itself resolved into nothingness, so also would the wound disappear'.*[105]

In 1894 *'The Spectator'* newspaper printed the following spell to charm handkerchiefs that were to be tied round the limbs of those suffering from a complaint called 'the white swelling'. The correspondent says that he '...*had it from the person who is in the habit of using it, who receives no money for doing so, and who is as firmly convinced of its efficacy as she is of her own existence.'*

'As Christ was walking he saw the Virgin Mary sitting on a cold, marble stone. He said unto her, What aileth thee, He said unto her, If it is a white ill-thing, or a red ill-thing, or a black ill-thing, or a sticking, cracking, pricking, stabbing

---

bone ill-thing, or a sore ill-thing, or a swelling ill-thing, or a rotten ill-thing, or a cold, creeping ill-thing, or a smarting ill-thing, let it fall from thee to the earth, in my name, and the name of the Father, Son, and Holy Ghost.
Amen. So be it.'

The charm is to be repeated nine times, and each time the Lord's Prayer is to be said. Another version is:

As our Blessed Virgin Mary was walking over along leading her youngest son by the hand he hang down his hed. "Why dew you hang down you're hed so low my son?" "my hed doth ake and all my bones." "I fear some ill things you have" I will bless you for ill things." (red ill, wite ill, black ill or blew or all other) down to the ground in the name of Lord Jesus Christ.
I bless thee [mention the name of the person] in the name of our Lord Jesus Christ,
Amen.

The Marystowe lady from whom this charm was collected states that '...*In using this the charmer must pass the hand the same way as the sun goes* [deosil]*, and pass it towards the ground.*' [106]

To Cure Inflammation 🌿
Say over the patient:

> *'The Queen of parest is gone into a far country to kill and destroy both men, women, and children, and then her meet our blessed Lord and Saviour Jesus Christ. He said "where are you going thou Queen of parest?" I am going into a far country to kill and destroy both men, women, and children." "Thou Queen of parest turn again: thy evil shall never do harm, in the name of the Father and of the Son, and of the Holy Ghost.*
> *Amen*' [107]

I can't help feeling that this strange charm from Devon is extremely old

---

106. *Devonshire Association Folk-Lore Transactions*, 1862 -1928
107. *Ibid*

and that something has been lost in repeated retelling. Who for example is the evil Queen of parest who is intent on killing people?

In his *'Healing Charms in Use in England and Wales 1700 to 1950'* the scholar and witchcraft expert Owen Davies comments that he has not come across examples of charms to cure inflammation outside the South West.

To Cure Whooping Cough ❦

Place some live spiders in a pouch and tie it around the patient's neck whilst saying:

'Spider as you waste away.
Whooping-cough no longer stay.' [108]

Or...

'procure a live flat fish — a little dab will do;
place it whilst alive on the bare breast of the
patient, and keep it there until it is dead'. [109]

---

108. Roper, Jonathan. *English Verbal Charms*, p. 153
109. Glyde, John. *The New Suffolk Garland*, 1866

Clearly in these charms the illness is being magically conveyed to the spiders or fish. The same theory also applies to this one:

> *'place a small piece of the child's hair between two slices of bread and butter. Give this to a dog to eat and the illness will be transferred to the dog.'* [110]

Or, if you don't want to give your dog whooping cough, give a saucer of milk to a ferret to drink then snatch the milk from it and give it to the child. The ferret must then be killed.[111] If you are reluctant to kill your ferret, you could try the more humane version of this spell given in A.R. Wright's 1928 leaflet *'English Folklore'*. Take some hair from the child's head, chop it fine and add it to milk. Divide the milk between the child and a ferret. I have also seen a Suffolk version of this charm recorded in 1866.[112]

---

110. Wright, R.A. *English Folklore*, 1928

111. *Ibid*

112. Glyde, John. *The New Suffolk Garland*, 1866

If it is your child that has whooping cough and you don't like the idea of transferring the ailment to an animal, try this remedy from 1877:

'Early, while the dew is on the ground, turn a sheep away from the place where it has been sleeping, and lay the child, face downwards, on the spot'.[113]

In Lancashire, the 'witches ladder' was also used to cure whooping cough. A string with nine knots tied upon it, placed about the neck of a child, is reported to be an infallible remedy for whooping cough.[114] I suspect that there was once a set of words that accompanied these instructions — in similar charms a rhyme is said as each knot is tied. Also from the same Lancastrian collector is this cure; pass the child nine times round the neck of a she-ass for the same effect.[115]

---

113. *Devonshire Association Folk-Lore Transactions,* 1877
114. Heywood, John. *Lancashire Folk-lore,* 1882
115. *Ibid*

In Suffolk, we are told that whooping cough is cured by obtaining some 'hodmidods', or small snails. These are passed through the hands of the invalids and then suspended in the chimney on a string, *'...as they die the whooping cough will leave the children'*. The collector of this charm also recalls that at Monk's Eleigh in Suffolk, a live frog was hung up a chimney, in the belief that its death by such means would effect a cure.[116] Examples of both of these charms are in the collections of the Museum of Witchcraft.

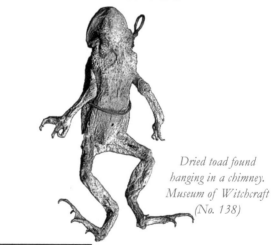

Dried toad found hanging in a chimney. Museum of Witchcraft (No. 138)

116. Glyde, John. *The New Suffolk Garland*, 1866

Stopping the Flow of Blood ✄

Hueffer quotes this charm in his *'Book of Witches'* (1908). He does not say where he collected it from but the spell also appears in *'Observations on Popular Antiquities'* accredited to an unnamed manuscript from 1475. It follows a very popular and ancient format:

> *Jesus that was in Bethlehem born and baptised was in flumen Jordane, as stinte the water at hys coming, so stinte the blood of thy Man N. thy servaunt throw the vertu of Thy Holy Name –Jesu - and Thy cosyn swete Saint Jon. And sey thys charme five tymes, with five Paternosters in worship of the five woundys.'* [117]

A similar version was collected in Polperro Cornwall:

> *'Our Saviour was born of Bethleam of Judeah. As He passed by Revoor of Jorden, the waters waid were all in one. The Lord ris up his holy hand. And bid the waters still to stan, and so shall the blood.* To be said three times'. [118]

---

117. *The Book of Witches,* 1908, p. 286

118. Couch, Jonathan. *The History of Polperro,* 1871

The river Jordan charm is possibly the most popular and widespread healing charm in Britain, and it is still in use today. Many variants can be found, but, when performing it, it is always spoken (sometimes whispered) and never written. It is often accompanied by actions such as placing a hand on the animal or person being healed. It is sometimes said that this charm will cure remotely, i.e. without the charmer visiting the patient.

Here are two more examples of this type of charm collected in the 19th and 20th centuries:

Jesus Christ was born in Bethlehem, and was baptised in the river Jordan.
The child was good
And the water stood
And so shall the blood
In the body of [person named three times][119]

Jesus was born in Bethlehem,
Baptised in the river Jordon, when
The water was wild in the wood,

119. *The Weekly Mercury*, 1883

The person was just and good,
God spake, and the river stood,
And so shall now thy blood [person's name]
In the Name of the Father, The Son, and of
The Holy Ghost.[120]

Whilst the river Jordan charm is very common, it is not the only magical solution to stop a wound bleeding. Say over the patient:

'In nominee Patris et Filii et Spiritus Sancti, carat, Cara, sarite, confirma consana imabolite'.[121]

'Septa + sepaga + sepagoga + Blood cease to flow. All is consummated in the Name of the Father + podendi + and of the son + pandera + and of the Holy Spirit + pandorica + peace be with you. Amen'.[122]

If you prefer to use English rather than Latin try:

---

120. *Devon & Cornwall Notes & Queries,* 1911
121. *The Book of Witches,* 1908, p. 286
122. *Ibid*

In the blood of Adam sin was taken,
In the blood of Christ it was all to shaken,
And by the same blood I do charge,
That the blood of N [name of person]
Run no longer at large.[123]

Or, to stop bleeding from arteries cut or bruised, repeat these words three times, desiring the blessing of God:

'Stand fast; lie as Christ did
When he was crucified upon the cross
Blood, remains up in the veins,
As Christ's did in all his pains!' [124]

To stop a nose bleed wear a skein of scarlet silk round the neck, tied with nine knots down the front. If the patient is male, the silk should be put on and the knots tied by a female, and vice versa.[125]

Yet again we see the use of the nine witch knots and red thread, or in this case a

---

123. Brant, John. *Observations on Popular Antiquities,* 1842
124. Glyde, John. *The New Suffolk Garland,* 1866
125. *Ibid*

red silk. You could, of course, use our old favourite:

> *Jesus came to the river Jordan and said, stand and it stood, and so I bid thee blood stand in the name of the Father, the Son and the Holy Ghost!*

The woman who used this particular version could apparently cure a nose bleed without having to leave home and visit the patient.[126]

To Cure Consumption

'*Strike* [touch or hit the patient] *with a piece of hempen rope with which a man has been hanged.*' [127] The recorder of this charm notes that ropes used by suicides had a marketable value, and that they were sold in one-inch lengths.

To Cure Erysipelas

All of the cures for this disease call for milk from a red cow. Get a little milk, from

---

126. *Transactions of the Penzance Natural History & Antiquarian Society,* 1888

127. *Devonshire Association Folk-Lore Transactions,* 1862 -1928

a red cow if you can, and while striking (touching) the diseased part say the prayer three times, and strike it around with the sun (clockwise or deosil):

Now come ye to the Lord of the land, Barney Fine. Barney Gout shall die away under a blackthorn, with red cow's milk and black wool.[128]

The use of the word 'strike' is interesting in these charms. Within witchcraft it is often associated with cursing – a person that has been cursed is sometimes said to have been 'struck'. In a healing context it could be seen as the disease being cursed and killed.

A report from Foxworthy in 1908 adds some more detail. Take the wool from under the left ear of a black sheep and the milk of a red cow. The wool is dipped in the milk every morning and used as a lotion.[129]

---

128. *Devonshire Association Folk-Lore Transactions*, c1894
129. *Ibid*, 1862 -1928

In 1906, Mrs Caunter from Dartmoor tells us:

You takes a piece of may [hawthorn] *and holds un in your 'and. Then you takes some milk from a red cow, an' some wool from a black sheep, an' strikes the place all one way. Then you hangs the pieces of may up in a chimney corner, tha do – an' when the may is withered the 'ary ciplis is gone. It cured'er!* [130]

To Cure a Sore Throat ✣
Take a piece of birch broom, and cross it nine times over the affected part.[131]

To Cure a Thorn Prick ✣
This charm from Mother Joan of Stowe was published in 1583. Say these words:

Our Lord was the first man
That ever thorne prick't upon:
It never blysted [blistered] *nor it never belted,*
And I pray God, nor this not may. [132]

---

130. *Ibid*, 1906
131. *Transactions of the Penzance Natural History & Antiquarian Society,* 1888
132. Brant, John. *Observations on Popular Antiquities,* 1842

A similar version, printed in Dyer's *'English Folklore'* in 1880 (300 years later) demonstrates the endurance of these old charms:

> *Our Saviour was of a Virgin born;*
> *His head was crowned with a crown of thorns;*
> *It never canker'd nor fester'd at all*
> *And I hope in Christ Jesus this never shaull*
> [shall].[133]

In Suffolk, the charm has the same opening lines followed by: *'He did neither swell nor rebel, and I hope this never will.'* Whilst reciting the above, the charmer must keep the middle finger of the right hand in motion around the thorn, and then touch it with the tip of their finger. *'Tis to be repeated three times and with God's blessing you will find no further trouble.'* [134]

A Southampton variant runs:

> *'Our Blessed saviour Came down from heaven,*
> *was pricked with a thorne, his blood went up*

---

133. Thiselton Dyer, T.F. *English Folklore,* 1880
134. Glyde, John. *The New Suffolk Garland,* 1866

to heaven again, his flesh neither kankered,
rankled, nor fustured, neither shall thine N
[name of injured person]'[135]

And in Norfolk they use:

Jesus of a maid was born,
He was pricked with nails and thorn;
Neither blains nor boils did fetch at the bone,
No more shall this, by Christ our Lord.
Amen.
So be it unto thee as I have said.' [136]

The last line of this version is
interesting in that it adds a definite point
at which the magic is done. In Masonic
ritual, and some witchcraft practices, the
expression 'So mote it be' performs a
similar function.

A more elaborate variant from Devon is:

'Our Savour Christ was Prick with thorns,
Never Rankled,
Never Fustered,

---

135. *Devonshire Association Folk-Lore Transactions,* 1862 -1928
136. Glyde, John. *The Norfolk Garland,* 1882

No more shant thine N [name of person]
Out of the Bone into the flesh,
Out of the fleash into the skin,
Out of the skin into the Earth.' [137]

Also from Devon:

'When Christ was upon middle earth he was
prick, his blood sprung into heaven.
It shall neither runkle, canker nor rust
neither shall thy blood (name the person)
in the name of the Father and of the Son and
of the Holy Ghost.' [138]

According to the *'The Book of Witches'*
(1908), a Mr. Smerdon had a thorn prick
cured by this charm being repeated three
times followed by 'Amen' and The Lord's
Prayer:

When our saviour Christ was on earth He
pricked his forefinger on the right hand with
a black thorn, or whatever it may be, and

---

137. *Devonshire Association Folk-Lore Transactions*, 1862 -1928
138. *The Devonshire Association for the Advancement of*
Science, Literature, 1899

the Blood sprang up to Heaven, nor moath, nor rust, nor canker did corrupt, and if Mr. Smerdon will put his trust in God his will do the same. In the name of the Father and of the Son and of the Holy Ghost.[139]

To Cure a Mad-Dog Bite ⚕

Write these words on a piece of bread: *Irioni Khiriori effera Kunder fere.* Then swallow the bread.[140]

Or, write the following on a piece of paper or bread then eat it:

Oh, King of Glory, Jesus Christ, come in peace in the name of the Father + max in the name of the Son + max in the name of the Holy Ghost, prax, Gasper, Melchior, Balthasar + Prax + max + Gods imax +.[141]

To Cure Epilepsy ⚕

This ancient charm dates back as far as the 12th century and is venerating the Christian magi (the three wise men) who

---

139. *The Book of Witches*, 1908

140. *Ibid*

141. *Ibid*

were of course magicians. It is interesting that the charm survived for hundreds of years in its Latin form. Say:

Gaspare fert myrrham, thus Melchoir, Balthasar aurum Haec tria cui secum portabit nomina regum Soluitur a morbo Christi pietate caduco.[142]

(Gaspar brings myrrh, Melchior frankincense, Balthazar gold, whoever carries with him these three names of the kings will be released from the falling sickness by the graciousness of Christ.)

It may be the incense that the three wise men were carrying that connects them with epilepsy; incense has often been used as a remedy for the condition. It has even been suggested that the connection may have come about from the biblical description of their actions; falling down they adored him. Epilepsy was known as the falling sickness, and it was a common belief that someone afflicted with epilepsy was possessed by evil spirits, or had been cursed.

---

142. *The Book of Witches*, 1908

Another cure for epilepsy is to hold the hand of the patient and say into his ear:

I conjure you by the Sun, the Moon, the Gospel of the Day, given of God to Saint Hubert, Gilles, Corneille and Jein, that you get up without falling again, in the name of the Father, the Son and the Holy Ghost. Amen [143]

A Scottish solution is: '*On the spot where the epileptic first falls, a black cock is buried alive along with a lock of the patient's hair and some parings of his nails.*' [144]

Thomas Davidson in '*Rowan Tree and Red Thread*' (1949), comments that the sacrificial nature of this charm is very thinly veiled indeed.

Yet another cure for epilepsy is to write the following, arranged in a square, on a piece of paper. Place the charm in a bag and hang it around your neck.[145]

---

143. *Ibid*, p. 284

144. Davidson, Thomas. '*Rowan Tree & Red Thread*', 1949, p. 48

145. K. I. Jones, *Folklore & Witchcraft of Devon & Cornwall*, 1997

Callen	Dan	Dant
Dan	Dant	Callen
Dant	Callen	Dan

A longer version of this appears in the commonplace book of William Sykes, schoolmaster of Crossland (near Huddersfield) in 1765. This charm was to cure someone who is...

'...*afflicted with an evil spirit, or witch, or wizard, or is forespoken by an evil tongue or an evil eye*'.

Callan Dan
Callan Dan Dant
Dan Dant Gallon
Gallon Dan Dallon Dant

Gallon Dan Dant
Dan Dallon
Dan Dant

'*It must be wrote on parchment and in a secret part sewed in their clothes; and the party that wears it must not see the writing, nor to know what is written. It must be carefully lapped up*'.[146]

To Cure Fits ❧

The afflicted person must beg a penny from thirty young people of the opposite sex. Then another person must change them for half-a-crown. This coin must be made into a ring without payment. The ring, if constantly worn, will quite cure fits. There was a report of this procedure in '*The Western Morning News*' in 1906. The woman with epilepsy sat silently in the porch of the village church during the sermon and twelve previously selected married men each put a penny in her lap after the service. The thirteenth man took the pennies and changed

---

146. *Folklore*, 1919

them for a half-crown from which the ring was to be made.[147]

Another version of this charm is recorded in 1866 in Suffolk. If a young woman has fits she applies to ten or a dozen unmarried men and obtains from them a small piece of silver of any kind, as a piece of broken spoon, or ring, or broach, or buckle, and even sometimes a small coin, and a penny (without telling them the purpose for which the pieces are wanted). The twelve pieces of silver are taken to a silversmith who forms them into a ring, which is to be worn on the forth finger of the left hand of the woman afflicted.[148] In Herefordshire you simply have to wear a ring made from a sacrament shilling.[149]

Florin Ring. The Museum of Witchcraft (No. 2039)

147. *Devonshire Association Folk-Lore Transactions,* 1862 -1928
148. Glyde, John. *The New Suffolk Garland,* 1866
149. Havergal, F.T. *Herefordshire Words, Superstitions & Customs,* 1887

By hand-beating the half crown or sacrament shilling, the text from around the edge of the coin was preserved on the inside of the ring.

To Cure Cramp ✲
Recite these words over the affected limb:

The cramp is keenless,
Mary was sinless:
when Mary bore Jesus,
let the cramp go away in the name of Jesus.[150]

Or, to prevent cramp, take the small bone of a leg of mutton, and carry it always about with you in your pocket.[151] Or, wear a ring made out of an old coffin handle on one finger. The collector of this charm notes that parish clerks have been known to preserve old coffin handles found in the church yard, for the purpose of making cramp rings.[152] Coffin nails, gold and silver, were also used to

150. Couch, Jonathan. *The History of Polperro*, 1871
151. Glyde, John. *The New Suffolk Garland*, 1866
152. *Ibid*

make cramp rings. Legend has it that one was given to Edward the Confessor by a pilgrim returning from Jerusalem, and it proved most efficacious. Cramp rings were also said to cure falling-sickness (epilepsy).

To Cure The King's Evil ✤

To Cure 'The King's Evil' or 'Scrofula', which is a form of Tuberculosis, pluck vervaine with the root, wrap in a leaf, and warm under cinders. This must be applied to the patient by a fasting virgin. The patient must also be fasting, and whilst touching the patient's hand the virgin must say: *'Appollo, let not the plague increase which virgin has allayed'*. She must then spit three times.[153]

To Cure a Headache ✤

Dry and powder the moss that was growing on a dead man's skull, and take it as snuff.[154] I think I would rather suffer the headache!

---

153. *The Book of Witches*, 1908, p. 284
154. Brant, John. *Observations on Popular Antiquities*, 1842

To Cure Boils ✄

Find a bramble that is growing on two men's land, i.e. the roots in one person's land and the bramble having grown over a hedge into the other's. Creep under the bramble three times and your boils will disappear.[155]

In a version of this charm from Mr Doidge of Great Torrington, he states that he had to crawl under a bramble 'the way of the sun' (clockwise or deosil), whilst fasting on three successive Sundays.[156]

In Suffolk the patient is...

'...to be dragged under a gooseberry or bramble, both ends of which are growing in the ground.'

This version is not specific to boils.[157] But this variant is:

'crawl backwards three times round a thorn bush very early in the morning, while the dew is on the grass.'[158]

---

155. *Devon & Cornwall Notes & Queries*, Vol. 6, 1911

156. *Devonshire Association Folk-Lore Transactions*, 1862 -1928

157. Glyde, John. *The New Suffolk Garland*, 1866

158. *Devonshire Association Folk-Lore Transactions*, 1906

To Cure Toothache

Say, *'Galbes, Galbat, Galdes, Galda'*[159] or, write the following on paper and hang it in a pouch, around the patient's neck:

> *Peter sat at the gate of the Temple, and Christ said unto him 'What aileth thee?' he said 'Oh my tooth!' Christ said to Peter, follow me and thou shalt not feel the tooth ache no more.*[160]

Or if you prefer to use Latin in your charms write *'Strigiles, falcesque, dentatae. Dentium, dolorem persanate'* on a piece of paper and hang it around your neck.[161]

Agrippa's solution seems rather cruel: *'...the tooth of a Mole taken out whilst she is alive, being afterwards let go,* [will] *cure the toothache.'* [162]

Many of the charms for toothache tell the story of Christ healing Peter. This was found in an old account book in a farmhouse in Marystowe, Devon:

159. *The Book of Witches,* 1908, p. 281

160. Couch, Jonathan. *The History of Polperro,* 1871

161. *The Book of Witches,* 1908, p. 281

162. Agrippa, 1533

'Peter stood by the gate of Jerusalem weeping, and the Lord said unto Peter, "Why weepest thou Peter?" an he said "Lord I am sore troubled with the tooth-ache that I know not what to do." The Lord God said "arise Peter and go with God, and I will help thee of tooth-ache." Grant Lord that she that is troubled thou may help them in the name of the Father an of the Son an of the Holy Ghost.' [163]

In Lancashire, we find a similar charm but with Peter sitting on a marble stone:

'Peter sat weeping on a marble stone. Jesus came near and said, "What aileth thee, O Peter?" He answered and said, "My Lord and my God!" He that can say this, and believeth it for my sake, never more shall have tooth-ache.' [164]

We are told by the authors of *Lancashire Folklore* (1882) that *'...Our wise men still sell the following charm ...but it must be worn inside the vest or stays, and over the left breast'.*

---

163. *Devonshire Association Folk-Lore Transactions*, 1862 -1928
164. Heywood, John. *Lancashire Folk-lore*, 1882

*Ass Sant Petter sat at the geats of Jerusalm
our Blessed Lord and Sevour Jesus Crist Pased
by and Sead, What Eleth thee hee sead Lord
my Teeth ecketh hee sead arise and follow mee
and thy Teeth shall never Eake Eney moor.
Fiat +Fiat +Fiat.*[165]

A Cornish variant of the charm is to
write this on paper:

*Peter sat at the gate of the Temple, and Christ
said unto him 'What aileth thee?' he said 'Oh
my tooth!' Christ said to Peter, follow me and
thou shalt not feel the tooth ache no more.*[166]

In Herefordshire a written version of
the charm runs:

*Crist met Peter and saide unto him Peter what is the
mater with thee. Peter saide lorde I am tormented
with the paine in the tooth the worme shall die and
Thou shalt live and thow that shalt have this in
wrightin or in memory shall never have Paine in
the tooth. Therefore believe in the lorde youre God.*

---

165. Heywood, John. *Lancashire Folk-lore*, 1882
166. Couch, Jonathan. *The History of Polperro*, 1871

This charm was written on a small piece of paper sealed with pitch. The recorder notes '*...the charm did not take effect as money, 6d., was paid for it.*'[167] This highlights the difference in regional traditions. In Lancashire, the charm is being sold by 'wise men' but in Herefordshire purchasing the charm renders it useless. The way around this seems to be for the recipients of the healing to secretly, and anonymously, deliver a food parcel or other goods of value to the charmer.

In Herefordshire, a favourite remedy for toothache is a little bag of unts' feet (moles' feet) hung over the mantle piece. *Thence in case of toothache they are taken down and worn around the neck.*'[168]

Mole's foot & tiny charm bag. Scarborough Museum

167. Havergal, F.T. *Herefordshire Words, Superstitions & Customs*, 1887
168. *Ibid*

Yet another way to cure your aching tooth was to quote John, ch. ix, and Exodus ch. xii from *The Bible*, and then touch your teeth during Mass.[169] Or, according to *'The New Suffolk Garland'* (1866) *'always dress and undress the left leg and foot before the right one.'*[170]

In 1914 *'The Crediton Chronicle'* reported that, rather than having a tooth pulled, local farmers would put their arms around an ash tree, make a slit in the bark where the fingers met, and place some hair from the back of their head into the slit.[171] Or, we are told that you can simply sit under an ash tree and cut your toenails.[172] Maybe these are forms of sympathetic magic; as the hair or toenails rot and disappear so does the toothache. Or possibly the toothache is transferred to the ash tree? Again and again in these ancient charms we find the ash tree (sometimes the mountain ash or rowan) is the recipient of human ailments.

---

169. *The Book of Witches*, 1908, p. 281

170. Glyde, John. *The New Suffolk Garland*, 1866

171. Wright, R.A. *English Folklore*, 1928

172. *Ibid*

To Cure Painful Breasts ✄

Catch two woodlice and eat them alive. W. Harpey who collected this charm in 1882 reported that a patient, following this treatment said, *'I was forced to try the woodlice sur; they were mortal nasty; I feel'd 'em crawlin' down my droat, but they've done me a sight of good, ees to be sure'*.[173]

To Cure Burn-Gout ✄

Say over the patient:

> *Three or four fair maidens came from divers lands crying for burn-gout*
> *aching, smarting, and all kinds of burn-gout*
> *they went to the burrow town*
> *there they had brethren three*
> *they went to the salt seas*
> *and they never more returned again*
> *her or she shall have their health again*
> *in the name of the Father, and of the Son, and of the Holy Ghost. Amen. So be it.*[174]

---

173. *Devonshire Association Folk-Lore Transactions,* 1882
174. *Devonshire Association Folk-Lore Transactions,* 1862 -1928

To Cure Warts

Ask an ash or rowan tree to buy your warts:

Ashen tree, ashen tree
Pray you buy this wart off me.[175]

Then pay the tree by burying a coin under it, or leave some bread or an apple lodged in its branches. Or, find an ash tree, which has its keys (seeds) and carve the initial letters of your christian and surname on the bark, count the exact number of your warts, and cut as many notches in addition to the letters as you have warts; as the bark grows up, your warts will go away.[176] Another method is to run a pin into each wart in turn, and stick the pin into an ash tree.[177]

In most wart charms, the warts are magically transferred to another host. In the above charms, an ash or rowan tree is the recipient, but there are plenty

---

175. The Museum of Witchcraft Library & Archives

176. Glyde, John. *The New Suffolk Garland,* 1866

177. Wright, R.A. *English Folklore,* 1928

of alternatives: Cut an apple in two, rub one part on the warts and give it to a pig to eat, and eat the other part yourself.[178]

Another version of this is to cut an apple in two, and rub each half on the warts, then tie the apple together again with a piece of string and bury it. As the apple decays so will the warts.[179] Or, *'take a number of small stones, one for each wart, and make them into a parcel, or put them into a bag and lose them.'* One way of losing them is to hitch the parcel upon the horn of a cow, and allow her to dispose of them.[180]

The Museum of Witchcraft has several examples of 'get lost boxes' in which were placed items such as these stones. These boxes were usually left at cross roads at midnight. Cecil Williamson, the late curator of the museum, always gave the warning *'never pick up a box or bag at a crossroads!'* Fred Rowland of Hartland

---

178. *Devonshire Association Folk-Lore Transactions,* c1900
179. *Ibid*
180. *Ibid*

tells how his brother once picked up a parcel of small stones, and within a few weeks had a large number of warts![181]

You could try picking a broad bean pod and rubbing the wart with the inner part of the pod. Bury the pod in the garden, and, as it rots, the warts will pass away.[182] Where the wart is to be transferred to meat, it is a usual requirement that the meat is stolen; 'steal a piece of beef from a butcher's shop and rub your warts with it: then throw it down the necessary-house [toilet], or bury it.' As the beef rots your warts will decay.[183]

A Suffolk variant of this charm is to *'...steal a bit of bacon, strike the wart with it and bury it at a four cross-ways.'[184]*

In Devon, we are told to *'get a strawmot* [straw] *with a knot in it for each wart. Take each strawmot and pass the knot over a wart several times without speaking, and then place it carefully on the table. This is repeated with*

---

181. *Devonshire Association Folk-Lore Transactions,* c1900
182. *Ibid*
183. Brant, John. *Observations on Popular Antiquities,* 1842
184. Glyde, John. *The New Suffolk Garland,* 1866

a fresh straw for each wart until all have been done. Bury the strawmots and as they rot the warts will go.' [185]

Many charms or charmers need to know the exact number of warts that are to be removed; an error here will render the charm useless. *'Tie knots in a string, one for each wart, and touch each wart with a separate knot. Then throw the knotted string away, without seeing where it goes; as it decays the warts will disappear.'* [186]

'Cut a nick or notch in an elder stick [or hazel in Devon[187]] *for each wart, touch each one with the notch and bury the stick without telling anyone of it.'*[188] Or, get the sap out of a burning green stick and rub it on the warts while it is hot; after three days the warts will go away and never come again.[189]

It is sometimes a requirement that the person whose warts are to be charmed does not thank the charmer, or pay him/

185. *Devonshire Association Folk-Lore Transactions,* c1870

186. *Ibid,* 1900

187. *Ibid*

188. Various. *Notes & Queries,* 1855

189. *Devonshire Association Folk-Lore Transactions,* c1900

her. A description of the wart charming process from Herefordshire runs: '... *she gathered some ears of wheat ripe, and with her hand full of corn crossed the warts several times. This done she wrapped up the corn into a packet, like that of a one oz. packet of tobacco, and dropped it where three roads met.*' He is certain that the warts disappeared at once and the person who picked up the packet of wheat is now the sufferer.[190]

There are so many wart charms in the records that one could dedicate a book wholly to the subject. Whilst many of the wart cures are self applied, or 'do it yourself' charms, there are also many wart charmers still plying their trade throughout Britain today. I have personally witnessed the process conducted in a Cornish Pub. I suspect however that some of the less pleasant methods of wart charming have died out: '*Get a black slug and slit it open to show the white inside, rub this over the wart, then pin the still live slug to a thorn tree during the new moon, or waning moon ...as the slug dries up*

190. Havergal F.T. *Herefordshire Words, Superstitions & Customs*, 1887

the wart will fall off and be gone by full moon.' This charm was collected in Cornwall by William Paynter.[191]

A similar charm recorded in Eastnor, Herefordshire, negates the need to slit open the slug, but suggests that you simply rub the wart with the large black slug then impale the creature on a thorn bush.[192] Another rather cruel wart charm is to hold a mole in the hand affected, and make its nose bleed; keeping it in the hand until it is dead.[193]

I was approached recently by a local builder asking if I could cure a large wart-like lump on his hand. I advised him to try my favourite wart charm. I told him to point at the wart and shout *'Fig I'* three times, pointing separately each time and laugh out loud. Within days the builder called by to show me his wart-free hand. In true Cornish tradition, the builder did not thank me but 'forgot' to send me a bill for some of the work he had recently

191. Semmens, Jason. *The Cornish Witch Finder*
192. Havergal F.T. *Herefordshire Words, Superstitions & Customs*, 1887
193. *Devonshire Association Folk-Lore Transactions*, 1883

undertaken for me. I 'borrowed' this
lovely charm from an Okehampton
collector who thought that *'Fig I'*
probably stood for *'Figs I say'* meaning
'I don't give a fig for you.'[194]

To Cure Corns

Take off your shoe and stocking when
you first see the new moon. Show
your corn to the new moon and say
'Corns down here; Narry waun up there.'
[195] Or, crush a little slug and put it on
the smooth side of an ivy leaf, then
put it on the corn.[196]

To Cure a Burn or Scald

Blow three times on the blisters, repeating
the words:

Here come I to cure a burnt sore
If the dead knew what the living endure,
The burnt sore would burn no more.[197]

194. *Devonshire Association Folk-Lore Transactions,* c1900

195. *Folklore & Witchcraft of the Cornish Village,* 2004

196. *Devonshire Association Folk-Lore Transactions,* 1907

197. Wright, R.A. *English Folklore,* 1928

This charm is also recorded in Scotland.[198] A more common charm involves angels arriving from various directions:

As I passed over the river Jordan,
I met with Christ, and he says unto me,
Woman what aileth thee?
Oh Lord my flesh doth burn.
The Lord saith unto me,
two angels cometh from the west,
one for fire, and one for frost,
out fire and frost in
in the name of the Father and of the Son and
of the Holy Ghost.[199]

A simpler version is:

There were three angels flying over the west,
One cried fire, and the other cried frost,
The other was the Holy Ghost.
Out fire, in frost,
In the name of the Father and of the Son and

198. Chambers, Robert. *Popular Rhymes, Fireside Stories,*
& Amusements of Scotland, 1842
199. Couch, Jonathan. *The History of Polperro,* 1871

of the Holy Ghost.
This must be repeated three times.[200]

Another variation of this charm is:

Three angels came from the north, east, and west,
One brought fire, and another brought frost,
And the third brought the Holy Ghost.
So out fire, and in frost,
In the name of the Father and of the Son and
of the Holy Ghost.[201]

A similar charm appears in *'Notes &*
Queries' (1855), in this version there
are only two angels and they come
from the east. A Suffolk variant has
two angels coming from the north. *The*
New Suffolk Garland' (1866) recorded
that *'one old woman, of very witch-*
like appearance, had great skill in curing
burns'.[202] Before uttering her charm
(probably a variant of 'three angels')
she prepared an ointment, and placed

---

200. *The Weekly Mercury*, 1883
201. Jones, K. I. *Folklore & Witchcraft of Devon & Cornwall*, 1997
202. Glyde, John. *The New Suffolk Garland*, 1866

some of it upon the part affected, then made the sign of the cross over it.[203]

To Stop Nightmares ❧

Hang a flint with a hole in it (a hag stone) on a string by the manger, or better still they say, hang it around your neck.[204] This charm is found throughout Britain and is said to work for animals, adults and children.

In Suffolk, we are told that, to prevent nightmares, before going to bed you should *'place your shoes carefully by the bed side "coming and going," that is, with the heal of one pointing in the direction of the toe of the other, then you will be sure to sleep quietly and well.'* [205]

Later, we will see a similar charm in which your shoes are placed in the form of a 'T' to induce dreams of a future partner. Shoes feature in many magical charms possibly because of their ability to hold the essence or spirit of the owner even when not being worn.

---

203. *Ibid*
204. Brant, John. *Observations on Popular Antiquities*, 1842
205. Glyde, John. *The New Suffolk Garland*, 1866

To Cure a Viper's Bite ✄

To cure a bite from an adder or other snake, apply toad's skin to the affected part. Tradition has it that toads are immune to viper bites.[206]

A rather strange set of instructions from Cornwall tells us to recite this over the snake bite:

'Bradgty, bradgty, bradgty,
under the ashing leaf.'

To be repeated three times and strike your hand with the growing of the hare.

I interpret this as meaning strike the wound with an ash twig with leaves attached during the waxing moon. The instructions continue:

'Bradgty, Bradgty, Bradgty, to be repeated three times before eight, eight times before seven, and seven times before six and six times before five and five times before four, four before three, three before two, and two before one and one before every one, three times for the bit [bite] *of an adder.'*

---

206. *Devonshire Association Folk-Lore Transactions,* 1862 -1928

This charm starts to make sense if we relate it to time, e.g. *'...repeat three times before eight o'clock, eight times before seven o'clock,'* etc. The author states that he *'...happed once on a manuscript account-book of a white witch or charmer... Risking the impropriety, I copied...'* [the above charm].[207]

Whilst these instructions are unclear to us, they remain interesting in several respects. Clearly it is unusual to find a spoken charm with no obvious Christian overlay. Also, the first part of the charm is to be undertaken under a growing moon. A waxing moon is often associated with healing and a waning moon with banishing. The multiple repetitions of the charm, diminishing through the day, are a classic banishing. In this case, it is ridding the body of the poison. So it could be said this charm works in two ways; banishing the poison from the body, and healing the wound.

---

207. Couch, Jonathan. *The History of Polperro*, 1871

To Cure Snake Bites & Insect Stings ⚓

The place affected must be struck three times with nine shoots of hazel twigs, the operator repeating three times in a breath:

Let God arise, and then His foes,
His enemies, for fear shall run.[208]

In Cumbria, it is said that, when a dog is bitten by an adder, the only remedy is to wash the place with the milk of an Irish cow. At Chatton in Northumberland, it is believed that if a native of Ireland draws a ring round a toad or adder, the creature cannot get out and will die there.[209] In other regions, simply drawing a ring around the adder with an ash or hazel wand will prevent it from moving.

To Cure Sciatica ⚓

This old charm for sciatica (lower back/leg pain) from Exmoor requires that the patient must lie upon his back on the

---

208. *Devonshire Association Folk-Lore Transactions,* 1862 -1928

209. Henderson, William. *Notes on the Folk-Lore of the Northern Counties of England & the Borders,* 1879

bank of the river or brook, with a straight staff by his side between his body and the water. These words are to be read over him:

Boneshave right
Boneshave straight
As the water runs by the stave
Good for Boneshave.[210]

In *'Criminal Trials in Scotland'* (1833) Robert Pitcairn writes, *'they are not to be persuaded but that this ridiculous form of words seldom fails to give them a perfect cure'*.

An account of the unsuccessful use of this charm is recorded in 1892:

Two women on opposite banks, with joined hands stretched over Jack and the stream, chanted in monotone;
"Boneshave right,
Boneshave strite
As tha watter rins by tha stave,
Zo follow boneshave."
Then they silently departed in opposite

210. Brant, John. *Observations on Popular Antiquities*, 1842

directions…Needless to state boneshave sticked to en, and ere daylight death had carried him away'.[211]

To Cure Thrush in a Child ❧

This charm was collected in 1898 by the Rev. Baring-Gould in Lew Trenchard. He writes that it was *'put into practice last week with complete success'.*

The babe is taken down to a willis (spring) and the child is held in the mother's arms under the spring, and its tongue is held down with the finger. Then the mother takes a long thread and lets it float down the stream towards her, then draws it through the child's mouth and round its head twice, and says over it the 8th psalm.

On the third morning after having done this, the thread is cast into the stream and allowed to float away with it.[212] I would have thought that the risk of drowning your child during this procedure would have deterred most mothers.

---

211. Hewett, Sarah. *The Peasant Speech of Devon,* 1892
212. *Devonshire Association Folk-Lore Transactions,* 1898

Springs and Holy Wells are often associated with healing. Usually the patient is taken to a Holy Well, and a strip of cloth is torn from their clothing close to the injury or ailment. This rag or 'cloutie' is dipped in the water then hung on a thorn tree over the well. Charms or prayers are said and the rag left to rot; as the cloth disintegrates the illness or injury will heal. Throughout Britain, but especially prevalent in Celtic regions, Holy Wells have become associated with curing particular ailments. Some, like St Winefride's in Flintshire, Wales, have a remarkable reputation for curing all problems. These ancient, sacred places have magical qualities that are still used today.

Sancreed Well with Clouties, 2013

To Cure Croup ❧

Coat shotgun shot in butter and give to the
patient to swallow.[213] I have often found lead
shot in my pigeon pie, but I am always careful
not to swallow it. As lead is poisonous I am
not sure if this charm would do more harm
than good.

To Cure Shingles or Girdings ❧

To cure a man, catch a black female cat and
cut off a piece of her tail (or ear), and collect
the blood in a saucer. Let the cat go and catch
a hen, cut the comb or wattles, and squeeze
out the blood into the same saucer. Next
find a woman who is suckling a female child,
squeeze out some of her milk into the same
saucer and stir.

To cure a female, substitute a tomcat for
the female cat, a cockerel for the hen, and a
woman suckling a male child for the woman
suckling a female child. The mixture is spread
over the eruption with a feather, and the whole
covered with a layer of 'raw head' (rawhide?).
G. Pycroft, the author of this piece writes
There is a right way of doing these things and a wrong,

---

213. *Devonshire Association Folk-Lore Transactions,* 1898

and the above is the right way.' He explains that *'it is often carelessly done, and the blood of the cat is applied pure and unmixed; no wonder it so often fails'.*[214]

A simpler method is to procure a bulrush; a big, female bulrush for a male patient, and a small, male one for a female patient. Draw the bulrush around the body by the right side and see that the patient is facing the sun. After it encircles the body, tie a knot in the rush and after some time burn it – the malady will die.[215]

To Cure a Stye

Obtain a pot-stick, (the stick used by a washerwoman to stir garments whilst boiling) and put it through a gold wedding ring. Holding the ring in one hand and the stick in the other, strike (touch) the eye with the stick and say:

Pot-ee, pot-ee
Why dist pote me?
To pote the wan out of thine'ee. [216]

---

214. *The Weekly Mercury,* 1883
215. *Devonshire Association Folk-Lore Transactions,* 1862 -1928
216. *Ibid,* 1880

Another widely believed cure for a stye is to rub it with a gold wedding ring – better still ask a widow to touch it with her wedding ring.[217]

Or, take a cat (if for a man a male cat, if for a woman a female cat) and strike (touch) the eye with its tail. Another variant is to give the stye nine strokes of a tom-cat's tail.[218]

A Scottish charm to cure a stye is to say:

Why came the one stye without the two styes here?
Why came the two styes without the three styes here?
Why came the three styes without the four styes here?
Why came the four styes without the five styes here?
Why came the five styes without the six styes here?
Why came the six styes without the seven styes here?
Why came the seven styes without the eight styes here?
Why came the eight styes without the nine styes here?
Why came the nine or one at all here?
Repeat Pater Noster nine times.[219]

217. The Museum of Witchcraft Library & Archives
218. *Devonshire Association Folk-Lore Transactions,* 1883
219. Carmichael, Alexander. *Carmina Gadelica,* 1900

Other versions of this charm reverse the sequence – they start with nine styes and end with one stye.

To Cure Unwell Children ⚘

Take some of the hair of the eldest child, cut it into small pieces, put it into some milk and give the compound to the youngest child to drink (and so on throughout the family). Or take some hair from the cross on the back of a donkey and, having placed it in a bag, hang it round the necks of the invalid children.[220]

To Cure an Infant of a Rupture or Hernia ⚘

Pass the child between the two halves of a maiden ash that has been split down the middle. The two halves must then be bound. As the ash halves grow back together so will the child be cured.[221]

A Cornish version is to pass the child through a slit in an ash sapling before sunrise whilst fasting – the slit must then

---

220. Glyde, John. *The New Suffolk Garland,* 1866
221. *Ibid*

be bound up and, as it unites, the malady will be cured. In Gloucestershire, the child is passed backwards and forwards through the arch of a bramble.[222]

The large volume of healing charms and spells collected, demonstrates that a considerable percentage of the work of the British charm-maker was curing ill health. For hundreds of years we have turned to magic to help keep us healthy and cure us from ill health. Maybe we are still using magic when we wish someone well.

222. Moore, Thomas. *The Treasury of Botany*, 1866

Curing Animals

Curing animals was, and in some regions still is, a major part of the charmer's work. Indeed, in many rural areas the charmer is still consulted by farmers before resorting to the (more expensive) vet. Many of the 'human charms' are/were used on animals and vice versa.

To cure cattle Bartie Paterson used the following charm in Scotland:

I charge thee for arrowschot,
For doorschot, for wombschot,
For liverschot, for lungschote,
For hertschote-all the maist:
In the name of the Father, the Sone, and the Haly
Ghaist. Amen.[223]

---

223. Davidson, Thomas. 'Rowan Tree & Red Thread', 1949, p 50

Geordie Archibald had a different charm for curing his beasts – this was only to be spoken, not written:

Three bitten has three bitten
The tongue, the ear, the heart, all the maist;
Three things must ye haill,
The Father, Son and the Halie Ghost.[224]

A similar charm was used by Christian Gow of Orkney:

Three things hath thee forspoken,
Heart, tung, and eye, almost
Three things sall the mend agane,
Father, Sone and Halie Ghost.[225]

A variant of these charms (used to un-bewitch a drink) is found in the confessions of Anne Whittle, who was hanged for causing death through witchcraft in the famous Pendle witch trials of 1612:

---

224. Ibid, p. 53
225. Ibid

Three biters hast thou bitten,
The hart, ill eye, ill tonge:
Three bitter shall be thy boote,
Father, sonne, and holy ghost A gods name.
Five pater-nosters, five avies And a creede,
In worship of five wounds
Of our lord.

For a Cracked Heel in a Bullock

Watch the creature until it lays down. When it stands up mark the spot where the bad foot touches the turf. Cut the piece of turf like a hoof and turn it topside down. This charm is also recorded in Devon in 1908 where the ailment is called a 'kebbit'.[226]

Capturing a footprint is also used in cursing magic – the footprint is believed to hold the essence of the person or creature to be harmed or healed.

To Stop a Horse Getting Fat

Strike the horse with mountain ash (rowan). J.H. Penhale from Torrington, who recorded this charm in 1883,

---

226. Bateson, J.K. *Moorland Mysteries,* 1925

also noted his father said that 'care' or mountain ash would be hung around the necks of animals 'to stop them getting worse'.[227]

To Stop a Cow Producing Blood ✒

To stop a cow producing blood in her milk (sometimes called red milk), take the key of a door and milk the cow through the bow or loop.[228] Another version of this charm suggests milking the cow through the spring of a pair of sheep-shears.[229]

To Cure Ringworm ✒

Take a pinch of soda and one of salt and put in a spoon. Pour boiling water on it and rub on the spot every day at noon, moving the hand sun-wise (clockwise or deosil) as you rub it in. C.E. Larther who recorded this spell wrote: 'Carried out strictly according to these instructions, the remedy was

---

227. *Devonshire Association Folk-Lore Transactions,* 1862 -1928
228. *Ibid,* 1908
229. *Ibid,* 1883

effective. It is the relic of Sun worship in the noon and sunwise.' [230]

Against Night-Riding Spirits ✠

In Suffolk it is confirmed that '...*a hag stone, with a hole through, tied to the key of the stable door protects the horses*... [from being ridden by] *...Pharisees or Fairies.*' [231]

In a rare 16th century book of remedies for horses entitled *'The Fower Chiefest Offices Belonging to Horsemanship, by Tho. Blundenill, of Newton Flotman, in Norffolke'*, the following curious charm is given as a remedy for horses affected with the nightmare:

Take a Flynt Stone that hath a hole of hys owne kynde, and hang it ouer hym and wryte in a bill:

In nomine patris, etc.
Saint George our Ladyes Knight,
He walked day so did he night
Until he hir found,

---

230. *Devonshire Association Folk-Lore Transactions*, 1862 -1928
231. Glyde Junior, John. *The New Suffolk Garland*, 1866

He hir beate and hir bounde,
Till truely hir trouth she
him plyght
That she woulde not come
within the night.
There as Saint George
our Ladyes Knight
Named was three tymes,
Saint George.

And hang this Scripture ouer him, and let him alone. With such proper charmes as thys is, the false Fryers in tymes past were wont to charme the money out of the playne folkes purses.[232]

I was talking to a local farmer in Boscastle who told me how he recently telephoned a local charmer and asked for his assistance to cure cattle with ringworm. The charmer asked the number of cattle affected and told the farmer he would cure them and all would be well. He worked them remotely – without visiting the farm. Some time later, on checking his stock the farmer found the

---

232. Lawrence, Robert. *The Magic Of The Horse-Shoe*, 1889

animals were free from ringworm apart from one – he then realised that he had given the charmer the wrong number – he had miscounted and was one short. The remaining animal was then charmed separately.

Dog's heart with pins
The Museum of Witchcraft (No. 518)

Cursing
& Removing Curses

It is said that one must know how to curse before one can cure, and there is plenty of historical evidence to demonstrate that the witches and cunning folk of old were often quite capable of both cursing and curing. In Roman Britain, curses were scratched on small sheets of lead, an example from the British Museum reads *'I curse Tretia Maria and her life and mind and memory and liver and lungs mixed up together, and her words, thoughts and memory; thus may she be unable to speak what things are concealed, nor be able...'*.[233]

---

233. The British Museum. 1934, 1105.1

After the inscription had been written the lead had been pierced seven times. Often these curses are rolled or folded and hidden in the house of the person to be cursed.

However, it is true to say that far more healing spells have survived than harming spells, and many magical practitioners made a living by specialising in the removal of curses. So evidence indicates that the work of the village wise woman or cunning man was usually to assist in the well-being of their customers, rather than cursing their enemies. But, whenever folk-magic or witchcraft is mentioned, it is the image of a wax doll (or poppet as they are sometimes known) thrust with pins that somehow seems to prevail.

In *'The Reader's Digest March'* (1941) an article entitled *'Hexing Hitler'* suggested that the public could make Hitler dolls and stick pins into them. It even includes a song that could be repeated during the ritual:

Istan, come and help us,
We are driving nails and needles,
We are driving pins and needles,

194

In to Adolf Hitler's heart.
We are driving nails and needles,
We are driving pins and needles,
Cats will claw his heart in darkness,
dogs will bite it in the night.

Hitler pin-cushion
Museum of Witchcraft
(No. 2184)

A contemporary letter in The Museum of Witchcraft archive suggests instructing the *International Ladies Garment Workers Union* on how to mass produce Hitler dolls for image magic. This would suggest cursing on a national scale which may seem a little surprising, but Hitler pin-cushions were commercially manufactured so that the public could stick a pin in Adolf Hitler's 'Axis.'

In the First World War, similar items depicting Kaiser Bill were also manufactured. Whilst these items are interesting and amusing, I wonder if the people who purchased and used them realised they were in fact using ancient and traditional image witchcraft?

The pamphlet *'News from Scotland'* (1590) describes how Agnes Sampson allegedly prepared a spell to kill King James VI of Scotland. She took a black toad and hung it by its heels for three days and collected the venom that fell from it in an oyster shell and kept it 'close covered' until a piece of cloth from the intended victim could be obtained. The leaflet states that a shirt, napkin, handkerchief or a *'peece of linnen cloth which the King had worne and fouled'* would do. Had she obtained this she could have *'bewitched him to death, and put him to such extraordinary paines, as if he had beene lying upon sharp thornes and endes of Needles'.* Agnes Sampson confessed under extreme torture and was eventually strangled and burned as a witch.[234]

It is recorded in Glanvill's *'Saducismus Triumphatus'* (1664) that in Somerset, Ann Bishop *'made a picture in blackish wax, which the Devil baptised as before by the name of Newton* [the person to be cursed]'. Thorns were then thrust into the image. The book contains several descriptions of this practice in which the Devil appears *'in the shape of a man in black'.* After the ceremony, at which the wax images were baptised by the devil, they ... *had wine cakes etc.*[235] This is a very rare description of a coven of witches meeting in England. The ceremonies described included music, drinking alcohol and cursing their enemies.

---

234. *News from Scotland,* trial pamphlet, 1591
235. Glanville. *Saducismus Trimphatus,* 1681

The book contains a unique woodcut image of the witches meeting the Man-in-Black in a grove of trees and presenting him with a wax doll (poppet), presumably for baptism.

There are also descriptions of the use of wax pictures (effigies) stuck with pins to 'take away' life in *'Satan's Invisible World'* (1685). These wax effigies were variously placed in a hole behind the fireplace, buried in the bed straw, or in one case *'bound on a spit and turned about before the fire'.*[236]

Witch presenting poppet to the Man in Black.
Woodcut from Saducismus Triumphatus, Glanvill, 1664

---

236. Sinclair, George. *Satan's Invisible World Discovered,* 1685

To Gain Revenge ✤

Rise before sunrise on a Saturday morning and cut a branch of a nut-tree whilst saying, *'I cut you, branch of this summer, in the name of him whom I mean to strike or mutilate'*. Then put a cloth on a table saying three times, *'In nominee Patris+ et Filii + et spiritus sancti'*. Then three times, *'Et incute droch, myrroch, esenaroth, + betu + baroch + ass + maarot'*. Finally say, *'Holy Trinity punish him who has harmed me, and take away the harm by your great justice + eson elion + emaris ales age'*, then strike the cloth.[237]

To Make Someone Lame ✤

Carefully watch where your intended victim places their feet, preferably when the ground is muddy and the footprint is clearly visible. After the person has passed, select a good left foot print and when no body is looking: *'Drive a red-hot nail into the person's left-foot-step* [footprint]*'*. This old spell was recorded in Exeter in 1696, and will apparently cause the victim's foot and leg to become *'red and*

---

237. *The Book of Witches*, 1908, p. 290

fiery' and will continue to work until the nail is removed.[238]

Some 200 years later, a variant of this was recorded when a witch named as Mrs D from Countisbury, *'having seen her neighbour entering the churchyard, took a hammer and new nail and drove it into the ground in his footprint, and until the nail was removed he could not leave the churchyard.'* [239]

Other methods of using footprints involve taking a wax cast of the print and driving nails into the cast, or digging out the turf on which the intended victim has walked. I find it interesting that some of these methods are also used by cattle charmers for healing various ailments.

To Kill an Ill-Wisher ✹

To kill someone who has ill-wished or overlooked your horse, cut out the beast's heart and stuff it with pins – the one who has overlooked it will die (the horse that

238. Various authors, *Notes & Queries*, 1855
239. *Devonshire Association Folk-Lore Transactions*, 1907

had been 'overlooked' would of course already be dead).[240]

T.Q.Couch, writing in 1880, confirms that a similar spell was in use. *'When an ox or other beast has died in consequence of the ill wish, it is usual to take out the heart, stick it over with pins and nails, and roast it before the fire until the pins and nails have one by one dropped out of it; during which process the witch is supposed to be suffering in mysterious sympathy with the wasting heart.'* [241]

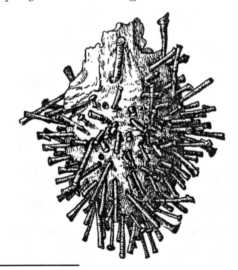

---

240. *Ibid*, 1862 -1928
241. Various authors, *Notes & Queries*, 1880

In Wales, to curse someone, one could go to the well at Ffynnon Elian in Denbighshire and *'put your enemy in the well'* – he or she would pine away or die. Putting your enemy in the well used to involve visiting the keeper of the well and having the name of the person (to be cursed) written into a register. The person's initials were written on a stone which was then cast into the well along with a pin. The practice continued well into the 19th century, but now the well is no longer accessible.[242]

The advent of photography was a gift to practitioners of the magical arts, indeed photography was in itself considered magical by many. A photograph captures the essence of a person much as an item of clothing, nail parings, or a footprint would. This old and tatty picture, found in the back of a filing cabinet, is now on display at The Museum of Witchcraft. The pins in it demonstrate a particularly nasty magical use of photographs.

---

242. Sykes, Wirt. *British Goblins,* 1881

Photograph with pins. Museum of Witchcraft (No. 40)

Removing Curses 🌿

To break the charm of bewitchment, a couple were told by a wise man who lived in Wells to sit in front of their fire at midnight and burn salt whilst remaining silent for one hour. Then they were to say:

This is not the thing I wish to burn
But [name of the curser] *heart of* [name of curser's village] *to turn*
Wishing thee neither to eat, drink, sleep nor rest
Until thou dost come to me and do my request

203

Or else the wrath of God may fall on thee
And cause thee to be consumed in a moment.
Amen

After this, the couple had to walk backwards to the stairs and climb them (still backwards), whilst reciting The Lord's Prayer backwards.

For the curse to be lifted, they were not allowed to speak another word until they were in bed.[243]

Many aspects of this charm are familiar to us, but here they are used in an unusual way. The basic *'not this thing I wish to burn'* is more commonly used in love magic i.e. *'It is not this heart I wish to burn but Mr Smith's heart I wish to turn'*. Burning salt is also sometimes associated with love magic, so this spell demonstrates that the magical power usually used to 'call to' or discover a lover can also be used against an enemy.

Reading The Lord's Prayer backwards is another traditional aspect of this spell, but one has to wonder if the God, whose

243. *Somerset & Dorset Notes & Queries, 1894*

wrath you are trying to send to the curser, might not be upset by this and decide to send a little wrath to the spell caster?

In Thomas Hardy's fictional story *The Return of the Native* published in 1878, he describes how, after making a beeswax image of Eustacia (the suspected evil-doer), Susan 'thrusted' it with pins and repeated The Lord's Prayer backwards three times along with the name of the wrong doer. Hardy writes that *'the incantation is usual in proceedings for obtaining unhallowed assistance against an enemy'.*

In 1926 it was reported that a woman in Norfolk whose husband was attracted by another woman, was told to keep The Lord's Prayer written backwards fastened under her blouse for three days a week. After a fortnight he would not recognise the other woman.[244]

To Un-Bewitch a Fishing Boat ⚓

If you are unable to catch fish when neighbouring boats catch hundreds... then it is known that your boat is *'witched'*.

---

244. Wright, R.A. *English Folklore*, 1928

A mackerel stuck with pins must be placed in the stern-hatch.[245]

The Witch Bottle ✀

To remove a curse using a witch bottle, put some of the bewitched person's water (urine) with a quantity of pins, needles, and nails into a bottle, cork them up and set them before the fire. A 1689 record of this procedure is very similar:

> *'stop the urine of the patient close up in a bottle, and put into it three nails, pins, or needles, with a little white salt, keeping the urine always warm.'*

The author says that the recipient of this spell will *'be grievously tormented, making their water with great difficulty, if at all'*.[246] Similar instructions appeared in *'The Daily Journal'* in 1731:

> *'a child being seized with strange and uncontrollable fits, the mother was advised*

---

245. *Somerset & Dorset Notes & Queries*, vol.10, 1906
246. Brant, John. *Observations on Popular Antiquities*, 1842

to hang a bottle of the child's water, mixed with some of its hair, close stopped over the fire, that the witch would thereupon come and break it.' [247]

A document from the late 18th century recently discovered in the Cornwall Record Office (see pages 69-70) is from a cunning-person to their client. It describes in detail the procedure to make and use a witch bottle, revealing that both the practitioner and the client were literate.

The main effect of a witch bottle was to prevent the wrongdoer passing urine, thus causing great discomfort and pain until the curse was removed.

Witches' bottles are often found walled up in old cottages, concealed in chimneys, or buried under a hearth; several examples of which are on display in the Museum of Witchcraft. In the 17th century, Bellarmine jars with their bearded masks were particularly popular vessels to use.

---

247. *The Daily Jouurnal,* 1731

To Un-Bewitch Someone ❧

Get a toad and pierce it on a board that is balanced in the middle of a log, then deal a heavy and sudden blow at the end of the board opposite to that on which is the reptile. This will send the toad flying into the air and is known as 'lifting the witch'.[248]

---

248. *Devonshire Association Folk-Lore Transactions*, 1862 -1928

Another method was observed by the folklorist Sabine Baring-Gould in 1879 in Chittlehamholt in Devon:

> *If one has been overlooked by a witch and is suffering in consequence, it is essential that three burning sticks be taken from the hearth of the overlooker, laid on the ground, walked over three times by the sufferer and then the fire should be quenched with water.*[249]

To Render a Witch Powerless

Procure some maiden nails from a blacksmith and drive them into the threshold of the witch's door – she will lose her power on crossing it. Alternatively drive the maiden nail into a place where the witch has placed her left foot – her power of mischief for the day is thus taken from her.

Maiden nails are those freshly made from bar-iron, and must never have been used. They must not be allowed to fall to, or be put on, the ground.[250]

---

249. Kinsman, John. *The Cornish Handbook*, 1931
250. *Devonshire Association Folk-Lore Transactions,* 1880

To Undo an Evil Spell

It is said that the power of evil ceases the moment blood is drawn from a witch.[251] This method of removing a curse is sometimes referred to as 'scratching' a witch and there are many recorded instances of women (witches) being scratched in the face with old nails or other sharp objects in the hope that a curse will be lifted. Belief that scratching will remove a curse is very old and widely held. In '*The Most Wonderful and True Stories* 1597':

> *'Some of the standers-by persuaded the boy to scratch her: which he did upon the face, and the back of her hands, so that the blood came apace: she stroked the back of her hand upon the child, saying: take blood enough child, God help thee. To whom the boy answered: Pray for thyself, thy prayer can do me no good.*
>
> *Here by the way, touching this use of scratching the witch: though it be commonly received as an approved means to descry the*

251. Couch, Jonathan. *The History of Polrerrow,* 1871

witch, and procure ease to the bewitched; yet seeing that neither by any natural cause, or supernatural warrant of God's word it hath any such virtue given unto it; it is to be received among the witchcrafts, whereof there be great store used in our land, to the great dishonour of God'.[252]

A modern method of rendering a person powerless over you is to place their photograph, wrapped tightly in white ribbon, in the back of your freezer.[253]

To Cure Bewitched People ✄

From the confessions of James Device in the famous Pendle witch trials of 1612:

Upon Good Friday I will fast while I may,
Untill I heare them knell
Our Lord's own bell.
Lord in his mess (feast)
With his twelve Apostles good,

---

252. Anon. *The Most Wonderfull & True Storie*, 1597
253. Collected from K. Godwin

What hath he in his hand?
Ligh (blaze) in leath (healing) wand:
What hath he in his other hand?
Heaven's doore keys.
Steck (fasten), Steck Hell door,
Let Chrizun child
Goe to its mother mild.
What is yonder that casts a light
so farrandly [pleasantly]*?*
Mine own dear Sonne that's naild to the tree.
He is naild sore by the head and hand;
And Holy harne Panne (skull).
Well is that man
That Friday spell can,
His child to learne;
A cross of Blue and another of Red,
As Good Lord was to the Roode.
Gabriel laid him down to sleep
Upon the ground of Holy weepe;
Good Lord came walking by,
Steepest thou, wakest thou Gabriel?
No, Lord, I am sted with stick and stake,
That I can neither sleepe nor wake.
Rise up, Gabriel, and go with me,
The stick nor the stake shall never deere thee.

With-ball, Gemma Gary

Mirrors are a simple and traditional way of reflecting evil back to its source and thus preventing and reversing curses. Reflective glass witch-balls were manufactured in England by Nailsea glass-makers from 1788 onwards. These would be (and still are) suspended in a window or dark corner where they reflect evil and ill-fortune.

When working with The Museum of Witchcraft, I was often asked for help by people who were convinced that they had been cursed. The museum archive holds documents that demonstrate that curses are not a thing of the past, there are people cursing and people removing curses in the 21st century. It is, however, interesting to note that there are far more beneficial than maleficent spells in this book and that balance is a true reflection of the museum's archive collection.

Spells & Charms in Songs

For she's gathered witch dew in the Kells kirkyard,
In the mirk how of the moon,
And fed hersel' wi' th' wild witch milk
With a red-hot burning spoon. [254]

Hidden amongst the wealth of traditional folk songs that have survived for hundreds of years are some magical gems. These songs have captured glimpses of the important part that magic, the witch, and her craft played in Britain in the near and distant past. Some of these are songs that clearly describe the spell-making process and others are, in themselves, musical charms; songs that are designed to bring about change through the act of singing. Indeed it could be said that all songs are spells – that all songs

---

254. M'Lehan. *Witchcraft and Superstitious Record*, 1911

effect change in the listener. However, the vast majority of magical songs describe the results achieved by the witch or spell caster. *'The Coal Blacksmith'* or *'The Two Magicians'*, for example, describe a magical seduction and chase in which the characters shape-shift into various animals:

Lady she's turned into a dove,
She flew up in the air;
He became a cock pigeon;
They flew pair and pair.

So the lady she turned into a hare,
She ran across the plain,
And he's become a grey-hound dog,
And he's fetched her back again.

Eventually the woman changes into a bed and the man gets his way:

So the lady she ran into the bedroom,
She changed into a bed,
And he's become her green coverlet,
Gained her maidenhead.[255]

---

255. *Songs of Witchcraft & Magic.* The Museum of Witchcraft

This song is possibly inspired by the Welsh tale of Taliesin, in which Ceridwen chases Gwion after he had drunk of the magical potion in her Cauldron of Inspiration.

In the chase, they both change (shape-shift) into various animals until, finally, Gwion turns into a grain of corn – Ceridwen turns into a hen and eats him.

In the 1662 trial of Isobel Gowdie, she confessed to changing into a hare and other animals:

I shall go into a hare
With sorrow and sighing and mickle care,
And I shall go in the Devil's name
Aye, till I come home again.

I shall turn into a cat,
With sorrow and sigh, and a black shot!
And I shall turn in the Devil's name,
Aye while I come home again.'

I shall turn into a crow,
With sorrow and sigh – and a black throw!
And I'll go in the Devil's name,
Aye while I come again.

In *'The White Goddess'* (1948) Robert Graves recognises the poetic quality of these confessions and concludes that they were originally from a witchcraft chase song like *'The Two Magicians'*. Graves goes a step further and 'reconstructs' the song;

Cunning and art he did not lack
But aye her whistle would fetch him back.

Oh I shall go into a hare
With sorrow and sighing and mickle care,
And I shall go in the Devil's name
Aye, till I be fetched home.

Hare, take heed of a bitch greyhound
Will harry thee all these fells around
For here come I in Our Lady's name
All but for to fetch thee home.

Cunning and art he did not lack
But aye her whistle would fetch him back.[256]

It is thought that 'fetching back' and 'fetching home' refers to 'changing back into human form'.

---

256. Graves, Robert. *The White Goddess, 1948*

The '*Laily* [loathsome] *Worm*' tells of a witch who turns her step-daughter into a fish and her son into a worm or serpent:

Oh I was scarcely seven years old when my mother she did die,
And my father married the worst woman that lived twixt the land and the sky.
For she's turned me into the laily worm that lies at the foot of the tree,
And my sister Maisry she has turned to the mackerel of the sea.[257]

Later in some versions of the song the spell is reversed:

Then she took up a silver wand and struck him three times three,
And that worm became the bravest knight that e'er your eyes did see.

In other versions the witch gets her comeuppance:

He has sent to the wood
For whins [gorse] *and for hawthorn*

---

257. *Songs of Witchcraft & Magic.* The Museum of Witchcraft

He has sent for his lady gay
And there he did her burn.

In 'The Broomfield Hill Wager', the heroine consults an 'old witch woman' who teaches her how to charm the local Lord to sleep so that she can win a wager by meeting him and returning with her virtue intact:

Up then spoke an old witch woman,
As she sat all alone,
Saying, 'You should go to the Broomfield Hill,
And a maid you will return.

And you'll pick the blossom from off the broom,
And the blossom that smells so sweet,
And you'll lay some down at the crown of his head
And more at the soles of his feet.

Then nine times did she go to the soles of his feet,
Nine times to the crown of his head;
And nine times she kissed his cherry red lips
As he lay on his green mossy bed.[258]

---

258. *Songs of Witchcraft & Magic.* The Museum of Witchcraft

One text makes it clear that strewing the broom flowers is part of the spell: *'And aye the thicker that ye do strew the sounder he will sleep.'* In all the many versions of this lovely old ballad, the woman keeps her virtue and leaves a token in the sleeping Lord's hand to prove she had visited and won the bet. In a song with a similar theme, *'The Maid on the Shore'*, the maiden is persuaded on board a ship and, before the captain could have his wicked way, she enchants the whole crew to sleep by singing her 'charmed' song, then she robs them.

She seated herself on the bow of the ship
And sang so low and sweet-O
One sang so sweet, genteel and complete
That she sang all the sailors to sleep,
She sang all the sailors to sleep.

She partook of his silver, partook of his gold,
Partook of his costly wearing,
She took his broadsword to make her an oar,
To paddle her back to the shore,
To paddle her back to the shore.[259]

---

259. Child, Francis James. *The English & Scottish Popular Ballads*, 1882-1898

Singing someone to sleep, singing a lullaby, is of course a form of enchanting – it is casting a spell.

In *'The Brown Girl'* our hero (the brown girl or country girl) is rejected by her posh lover in favour of a 'fair pretty maid'. Naturally the brown girl curses the two-timing Lord who falls ill:

At first he sent for the doctor-man,
Saying, 'Doctor you must me cure;
These pains that I do feel within
I cannot long endure.'

But nary a bit that doctor-man
his suffering could relieve;
No nary a one but the brown, brown girl
His life she would revive.

So the lord sends for the brown girl to come
and save his life, she walks ('walked and never
ran') up to him and laughs;

She took a white wand in her hand,
She strake him on the breast:
'I give thee back thy love and troth,
So may thy soul have rest.'

Having waved her magic wand and cast her spell to finish him off she proceeds to dance on his grave!

'O never will I forget, forgive,
Never will I forgive;
I'll dance, I'll dance on the green, green grass,
While you do lie beneath!' [260]

Whilst we should not take the above stories literally, there are aspects of the narratives that illustrate popular belief of the time. It is especially interesting that the lords and knights and sea captains were defeated by a country girl and an 'old witch woman'. A lesson may be learnt here – never cross a seemingly simple country person, they may well have a deep knowledge of the old ways!

'The Bitter Withy' depicts the young Jesus Christ as a magician, and tells how he used magic to make a bridge from sunbeams. He then collapses the bridge, deliberately drowning some rich children who wouldn't play with him:

---

260. *Songs of Witchcraft & Magic.* The Museum of Witchcraft

He's made him a bridge of the beams of the sun,
And over the river ran he;
And the rich young lords ran after him
And drowned they were all three.

On finding out about this incident, Christ's mother Mary rebukes him and beats him with willow twigs (withys) so Jesus curses the tree:

'Oh bitter withy! Oh bitter withy!
You have caused me to smart
And the willow shall be the very first tree,
To perish at the heart!' [261]

Yet again we find the working class (Jesus, son of a carpenter) defeating the aristocracy (the rich young lords) with the aid of spells and charms.

The old ballad *'Willie's Lady'* appears in Francis James Child's collection *'The English and Scottish Popular Ballads'* published in the 1880s. Willie's wife has been bewitched by his mother so that she cannot give birth. Using a wax effigy of

---

261. *Songs of Witchcraft & Magic.* The Museum of Witchcraft

a child, the witch mother is fooled into
revealing the spells she has used. It is
very rare for a folk song to record spell
craft in such detail but *'Willie's Lady'* is
an exceptional song. The spells included
'braiding nine witch knots in amongst this lady's
locks', braiding *'combs of care'* in amongst
this lady's hair, placing a *'master kid'* (goat)
that fed and slept all beneath this lady's
bed and lacing a charm into her left shoe.

King Willie he sailed over the raging foam,
He's woo'd a wife and he's brought her home.
He woo'd her for her long golden hair.
His mother wrought her a mighty care,
And a weary spell she's laid on her:
She'd be with child full long and many's the year,
But a child she would never bear.
And in her bower she lies in pain;
King Willie at her bed head he do stand,
As down his cheeks salten tears do run.
King Willie back to his mother he did run,
And he's gone there as a begging son.
'There's me true love has this fine noble steed,
The like of which you ne'er did see.
At every part of this horse's mane
There's hanging fifty silver bells and ten,

There's hanging fifty bells and ten.
This goodly gift shall be your own,
If back to me own true love you'll turn again
That she might bear her a baby son.'
'Of a child she'll never lighter be,
Nor from sickness will she e'er be free,
But she will die and she will turn to clay,
And you will wed with another may [maid].'
But sighing says this weary man,
As back to his own true love he's gone again,
'I wish my life was at an end!'
King Willie back to his mother he did run,
And he's gone there as a begging son.
Says, 'Me true love has this fine golden girdle
Set with jewels all about the middle.
At every part of this girdle's hem
There's hanging fifty silver bells and ten,
There's hanging fifty bells and ten.
This goodly gift shall be your own,
If back to me own true love you'll turn again
That she might bear her baby son.'
'Of a child she'll never lighter be,
Nor from sickness will she e'er be free,
But she will die and she will turn to clay,
And you will wed with another may.'
But sighing says this weary man,
As back to his own true love he's gone again,

'I wish my life was at an end!'
But up and spoke his noble Queen
And she has told King Willie of a plan,
How she might bear her baby son.
She's said,
'You must go get you down to the market place,
And you must buy you a loaf of wax;
And you must shape it as a babe that is to nurse,
And you must make two eyes of glass.
Ask your mother to a christening day,
And you must stand there, close as you can be,
That you might hear what she do say.'
King Willie he's gone down to the market place,
And he has bought him a loaf of wax;
And he has shaped it as a babe that is to nurse,
And he has made two eyes of glass.
He asked his mother to a christening day,
And he stood there close as he could be,
That he might hear what she did say.
And how she stormed and how she swore!
She spied the babe where no babe could be before.
She spied the babe where none could be before.
Says, Who was it who undid the nine witch knots
Braided in amongst this lady's locks?
And who was it who took out the combs of care
Braided in amongst this lady's hair?
And who was it slew the master kid

That fed and slept all beneath this lady's bed,
That ran and slept all beneath her bed?
And who was it unlaced her left shoe?
And who was it that let her lighter be,
That she might bear her baby boy?'
And it was Willie who undid the nine witch knots
Braided in amongst this lady's locks.
And it was Willie who took out the combs of care
Braided in amongst this lady's hair.
And it was Willie the master kid did slay,
And it was Willie who unlaced her left foot shoe,
And he has let her lighter be.
And she has born her a baby son,
And great are the blessings that be them upon,
And great are the blessings them upon.[262]

The 'nine witch knots' are of course the basis of the familiar 'witches' ladder'. Whilst the concept of knot magic is extremely old, the expression 'witches' ladder' appears to have been coined after the discovery of a string with feathers stuck into it hanging in an attic in Somerset in 1879. This charm is now on display in the excellent Pitt Rivers

262. *Songs of Witchcraft & Magic*. The Museum of Witchcraft

Museum in Oxford. The use of knots is very common in British spell-craft. 'Combs of care' may be combs of rowan wood as 'care' is a West Country name for rowan. We have already seen that rowan is considered to be a particularly potent and magical wood, but it is usually associated with protection. Presumably the 'master kid' was placed in a byre below the bedroom. Goats have a long association with magic and witchcraft, but this usage is unusual – possibly the goat was charmed or bewitched before being placed there. Elsewhere in this book you will find charms associated with the left foot or foot print – here the witch uses the left shoe. We do not know what charm was laced into the shoe, but as has already been demonstrated it is likely to have involved knots.

Apart from the spells detailed, the song is littered with hints of magical usage and magical imagery. The use of a wax doll or poppet to trick the mother into revealing the spells is ironic – the witch mother would, I am sure, have been very familiar with the use of poppets in cursing magic.

These Scottish rhyming cantrips (spells) describe how to prepare love potions. One can imagine the witches huddled over the steaming cauldron brewing up their magic!

In the pingle or the pan,
Or the haurnpan (skull) o' man,
Boil the heart's-bluid o' the tade [toad],
Wi' the tallow o' the gled;
Hawcket kail and hen dirt,
Chow'd cheese and chicken-wort;
Yallow puddocks champit sma',
Spiders ten and gellocks twa;
Sclaters twall, frae foggy dykes,
Bumbees twunty, frae their bykes;
Asks frae skinklin' lochans blue,
Ay, will mak' a better stue:
Bachelors maun hae a charm,
Hearts they hae fu' o' harm:
Ay the aulder, ay the caulder,
Ay the caulder, ay the baulder,
Traps sna' white, and tails green,
Snappin' maidens o' fifteen;
Mingle, mingle, in the pingle,
Join the cantrip wi' the jingle;
Now we see and now we see,
Plots o' paachin' ane, twa, three.[263]

263. *The Scots Magazine,* 1824

'Yirbs for the blinking queen,
Seeth now, when it is e'en,
Boortree branches, yellow gowans,
Berry rasps and berry rowans;
Deil's milk frae thrissles saft,
Clover blades frae aff the craft;
Binwud leaves and blinmen's baws,
Heather bells and wither'd haws;
Something sweet, something soor,
Time about wi' mild and door;
Hinnie-suckles, bluidy-fingers,
Napple roots and nettle stingers,
Bags o' bees and gall in bladders,
Gowks' spittles, pizion adders:
May dew and fumarts' tears,
Nool shearings, nowt's neers,
Mix, mix, six and six,
And the auld maid's cantrip fix.[264]

'The Bold Astrologer' is an amusing song which gives us a snap-shot of the world of the 19th century cunning man. Telling fortunes was one of their main services, and knowing what the future had in store was important, especially

228. *The Scots Magazine*, 1824

for young women. I am sure that the 'bold astrologer' had plenty of clients to practice his 'charming' techniques on:

There was a bold astrologer, in London he did dwell;

At telling maidens' fortunes, there's none could him excel

There was a pretty serving maid a-dwelling there close by;

She went one day to the astrologer and swore she'd have a try.

'I hear that you tell fortunes, sir. Would you tell me mine?' said she.

'Oh yes, fair maid, without a doubt, if you'll step upstairs with me.'

'To step upstairs with you, kind sir, I really am afraid!'

She spoke it in such modesty, as though she were a maid.

'To step upstairs with me, my dear, you need not be afraid,

Knowing 'twas but the other day you with your master laid.'

Then she began to curse and swear she would her master bring,

As witness both by him and her that they did

no such thing.
'Oh no, me dear, don't swear and curse – you'll
make the deed the worse;
For the gold piece that he gave to you, you've
got it in your purse.'
'Indeed you can tell fortunes, sir – you've told
me mine,' said she,
Then she drew out the gold piece; 'Good
morning, sir,' quoth she.

Many songs simply call for good luck to be granted to those present, but some are dedicated to specific tasks. In the Scottish Isles songs were sung whilst making cloth, especially during the waulking (thickening and softening) process. These songs often included a magical blessing. This one is from the wonderful collection *'Carmina Gadelica'* by Alexander Carmicheal (1900). Whilst something is always lost in translation, I hope you agree with me that this is simply magical:

Is math a ghabhas mi mo rann,
A teurnadh le gleann;
Aon rann,

235

Da rann,
Tri rann,
Ceithir rann,
Coig rann,
Sia rann,
Seachd rann,
Seachd gu lath rann
Seachd gu lath rann.
Nar a gonar fear an eididh,
Nar a reubar e gu brath,
Cian theid e 'n cath no 'n comhrag,
Sgiath chomarach an Domhnach da,
Can theid e 'n cath no 'n comhrag,
Sgiath chomarach an Domhnach da.
Chan ath-aodach seo, 's chan fhaoigh e,
'S cha chuid cleir no sagairt e.
Biolair uaine ga buain fo
'S air a toir do mhnai gun fhiosd;
Lurg an fheidh an ceann an sgadain,
'S an caol chalp a bhradain bhric.

Well can I say my rune,
Descending with the glen;
One rune,
Two runes,
Three runes,
Four runes,

236

Five runes,
Six runes.
Seven runes,
Seven and a half runes,
Seven and a half runes.
May the man of this clothing never be wounded,
May torn he never be;
What time he goes into battle or combat,
May the sanctuary shield of the Lord be his.
What time he goes into battle or combat,
May the sanctuary shield of the Lord be his.
This is not second clothing and it is not thigged,
Nor is it the right of sacristan or of priest.
Cresses green culled beneath a stone,
And given to a woman in secret.
The shank of the deer in the head of the herring,
And in the slender tail of the speckled
salmon.[265]

By blessing or consecrating the cloth with song, the waulkers are giving the clothing the qualities of an amulet – to wear a coat made from such cloth would be to wear magical protection and good fortune.

---

265. Carmichael, Alexander. *Carmina Gadelica*, 1900

A Magical Medley of
Spells & Charms

S pells and charms have been used to influence every situation imaginable, and in all classes of society. In 1926, Prime Minister Stanley Baldwin described this traditional ritual: *'On the day that I was born, our cook...wrapped me in a blanket, and to ensure that I should rise in life she did the proper thing – she carried me up some stairs. But she wanted my life to be a considerable one, so she tramped up to the top of the house, and when she got there she put a chair in the middle of one of the attic rooms, got on it with me in her arms, and then held me up'.*[266] Clearly this sympathetic magic worked well!

---

266. Glyde Junior, John. *The New Suffolk Garland*, 1866

If you want to have a child, rocking an empty cradle is sure to attract a baby to a childless home.[267] When the Museum of Witchcraft first opened in The Isle of Man, it exhibited an empty cradle to demonstrate this tradition. Many of the visitors tried the spell and rocked the cradle. Some fifty years later the museum still gets visitors who explain how they, or their mothers, became pregnant after doing so.

To Ease Childbirth ✄

Without the patient's knowledge, place in their bed a stone or dart that has caused the death of a man, a boar, or a bear, with one blow, and the travail will be easy and quick.[268] Or, place an *'Airne Mhoire'* in the hand of the expectant mother who must clasp it tight to ease the pain of child birth. The Airne Mhoire is a nut that has been carried across the Atlantic on the Gulf Stream and cast ashore. These exotic nuts are found in Scotland, Ireland

---

267. Wright, R.A. *English Folklore,* 1928
268. *The Book of Charms and Ceremonies,* 1910

and Cornwall, but they are scarce and
have always been considered very special
and magical. The nuts have a pronounced
cross on them, and are considered
especially potent in the Scottish Isles if
they are blessed in church by a Catholic
Priest. I am told that in Ireland they are
sometimes used to help teething children.
They are sometimes called Mary nuts,
Virgin nuts, or Mary beans and can be
worn as a protective amulet on a string
around one's neck.[269] The Museum of
Witchcraft has examples of these 'sea
beans' on display.

To Bless a Child with the Gift of Song ❧
To ensure that your new arrival becomes a
good singer remember to bury the child's
first nail-parings under an ash tree.[270]

For a Good Night's Sleep ❧
Use this old night blessing from the
Scottish Isles:

269. McNeill, F. Marian. *The Silver Bough*, 1956
270. Wright, R.A. *English Folklore*, 1928

A Dhe nan Dùl rinn iùl duinn thar a'chuan,
Thoir duinna nis sèamh-shuain fo sgéith do
ghràidh

King of the Elements, our guide across the sea,
Grant us now soft sleep beneath thy wing of
love.[271]

To Secure the Purchase of a House or Land ❧

Plant leek seeds around the house or
land that you wish to acquire. This spell
was passed to me by a wise friend who
has now passed away. It has helped me,
and others, on several occasions and
has proved to be especially effective in
house auctions. One local resident who
used this charm complains that he still
has leaks growing all around his garden.
'I can't get rid of the blooming things', he says
– a small price to pay to live in the home
of your dreams.

To Sell Your House ❧

There is a folk tradition that Saint Joseph
can help you. The tradition appears to

---

271. Macleod, Kenneth. *The Road to The Isles*, 1927

have originated in North America in the 1980s, but is now widespread in Britain. However, the charm incorporates many much older practices and is unusual in that if the Saint does not help quickly he is punished by being buried until the house is sold. Joseph is the patron saint of homes and family. His trade was that of a carpenter and house builder.

Stand a Saint Joseph figure in a prominent position in the house you want to sell, and give him treats i.e. candles, flowers, food, etc. You may also choose to paint your figure in bright colours. Every day, ask for help selling your house reciting:

Blessed Joseph, who was the guardian of Our Lady the Queen of Heaven and the Christ Child, who was warned by an angel of the danger to them from King Herod, and took them to safety in Egypt, please look with sympathy on my need to move house and to sell my property at [address], *and help me to achieve a quick and successful sale.*

If after one month your house has not sold, bury your Saint Joseph figure upside down in the garden of your house. Mark the position of the burial. When your house sells, remove Joseph, thank him, and give him a prominent position in your new home. There are many variations of this procedure – some suggest you do not wait the month before burial, some specify that the figure must be buried facing away from the house, but they all insist that he is buried upside down.[272]

To Prevent Saddle Sores 🌿

In Wiltshire, it is generally said that if a man takes an elder-stick and cuts it on both sides (so that he preserves the joint), and puts it in his pocket when he rides a journey, he shall never gall.[273] Richard Flecknoe's *'Diarium'* of 1658 confirms this charm but this time with alder wood:

How Alder-stick in pocket carried
By horseman who on highway feared,

---

272. Traditional. The author
273. Aubrey, John. *Remaines of Gentilisme & Judaisme,* 1686-87

His breech should n'ere be gall'd or wearied
Although he rid on trotting horse.[274]

But be careful if harvesting an elder-stick for this spell, as it is considered very unlucky and a 'wicked wrong' for anyone to harm an elder. In tradition the arboreal spirit known as the 'elder mother' lives in the tree and she will wreak havoc if upset.[275]

To Stop a Horse from Hurting You ✻

J.K. Bateson was told by his henchman that a foal is born with a complete set of teeth, and to preserve the tongue, nature provides a false tongue which is discarded as soon as the foal is born. Hang the false tongue on a blackthorn in bloom until it is quite dry. Grind the tongue to a powder with a flint. If carried with you always, no horse can harm you by tooth nor hoof.[276]

---

274. *Richard Flecknoe's Diarium,* 1658
275. Howard, Michael. *A Witch's Herbal,* 2012
276. Bateson, J.K. *Moorland Mysteries,* 1925

To Stop Witches Spiriting Away Milk ✄

Make a hoop three to four inches in diameter, of intertwined milkwort, butterwort, dandelion and marigold and bind it with a triple cord of lint. Place it under the milk vessel in the name of the Father, Son and Spirit.[277]

To Get Rid of Numerous Parasites ✄

Send a friend, or the town crier, to shout near the door of the witch (who you think has sent the curse), *'Take back your flock! Take back your flock!'* [278]

To Stop Caterpillars Eating Your Crops ✄

Address the creature saying:

> *'beloved caterpillar, this meat that you are having in the autumn profits you little as it profits the Virgin Mary when, in eating and drinking, people do not speak of Jesus Christ. In the name of God.*
> *Amen.'*

---

277. McNeill, F. Marian. *The Silver Bough,* 1956
278. Various authors. *Notes & Queries,* 1855

Or, to rid your cabbage patch of caterpillars, pick a switch (stick or wand) from close to an adulterer's house or the house of an upright magistrate. Walk straight across the cabbage-bed whilst striking an infected cabbage with the switch. Providing that you don't turn around, the caterpillars will faint and fall away![279] This is a very unusual charm and it seems to imply that the essence of both adulterers and upright magistrates have the ability to kill caterpillars – I have not come across anything similar.

Quarrelsome Neighbours

To protect quarrelsome neighbours from harming each other, place a horse-shoe between their houses and neither will incur any risk of evil as a result of the other's ill-wishes.[280]

Against Vermin & Foxes

To protect chickens and other animals from vermin and foxes, use this ancient charm:

With blessynges of Saynt Germayne
I wyll me so determine

---

279. *The Book of Witches*, 1908
280. Lawrence, Robert. *The Magic Of The Horse-Shoe*, 1889

That neyther fox nor vermyne
Shall do my chykens harme,
For your Gese eske Saynt Legearde,
For your Duckes Saynt Leonard
For Horse take Moyses yearde,
There is no better charm.[281]

To Make Butter 'Come' When Churning

Come, butter, come
Come, butter, come;
Peter stands at the gate,
Waiting for a butter'd cake;
Come, butter, come.[282]

To Keep Your Bees

Always inform your bees of the death of the head of your family by gently tapping on the hive and saying:

Bees, bees, awake!
Your master is dead
And another you must take.[283]

---

281. Brant, John. *Observations on Popular Antiquities*, 1842
282. Sinclair, George. *Satan's Invisible World Discovered*, 1685
283. *The Gentleman's Magazine*, 1810

I have personal knowledge that this has survived into the 20th century in Hampshire. In the village of Penton Mewsey, the bees were told of births, deaths and marriages. The village 'bee man' would visit the hives dressed in mourning hat and tails on the morning after a death and he would convey the news to each hive of bees. This is also recorded in Suffolk where *'the bees are said to be so sensitive as to leave a house if the inmates of which indulge habitually in swearing'.*[284]

In Devon, following a family death, the hives were *'put in mourning lest the bees should die'*. The record also recalls a case where thirty hives were *'tied up with crape because of a death'.*[285]

Rudyard Kipling describes the same tradition in his 'Bee Boy's Song':

Marriage, birth or buryin',
News across the seas,
All you're sad or merry in,
You must tell the Bees.

284. Glyde Junior, John. *The New Suffolk Garland*, 1866
285. *The Folk-Lore Record*, 1882

Kipling also included a verse about Brides:

A maiden in her glory,
Upon her wedding day,
Must tell her Bees the story,
Or else they'll fly away.
Fly away – die away –
Dwindle down and leave you!
But if you don't deceive your Bees,
Your Bees will not deceive you.

A Charm for Fishermen ❧

Stolen hook and
Hairy line and
Crooked rod of
Rowan wood
New found on shore-land
On the Lord's day.

Wind from homeland!
Out to sea ye!
Love of Colum!
Love of Clement!
Sure to-night we'll light up Rodel.
Hook a ree-oo

Hook a ree-oo
Hook a ree-oo
Ee-oo, ee-oo.[286]

This enchanting charm is from Rodel in Scotland. Like so many ancient charms and songs its literal meaning has been lost in the mists of time but its magic remains. The repeated vowel sounds and references to a crooked rod of rowan wood (a wand) clearly hint at magical ritual.

For Good Seas and Tides 🌾
Say this rune of the moon:

Hail to thee, thou new-lit moon,
I bend the knee, thou queen so fair;
Through the dark clouds thine the way be,
Thine who leadest all the stars;
Though thy light e'en find me joy-filled
Put thou flow-tide on the flood
Send thou flow-tide on the flood.[287]

---

286. Macleod, Kenneth. *The Road to The Isles,* 1927
287. Macleod, Kenneth. *The Road to The Isles,* 1927

To Prevent Drowning at Sea ❧

Carry a baby's caul with you. During childbirth some children's heads are covered with a membrane known as a caul. The belief that a caul will protect you from drowning is widespread amongst fisher-folk even today. An example may be seen in the Museum of Witchcraft's 'sea witchcraft' display.

Framed Caul. The Museum of Witchcraft (No. 272)

In *'David Copperfield'*, Charles Dickens wrote: *'I was born with a caul, which was advertised for sale, in the newspapers, at the low price of fifteen guineas. Whether sea-going people were short of money about that time, or were short of faith and preferred cork jackets, I don't know....'* [288]

To be born with a caul is also said to give you the ability to read palms and tell fortunes.

To Raise the Wind

Say this charm whilst 'knocking' a cloth against a stone:

I knock this rag upon this stone
To raise this wind in the Devils name
It shall not lie till I please again.[289]

To Capture the Wind

Stand on a hilltop on a windy day and catch three gusts of wind in separate knots of a cord or rope. This rope can then be sold to sailors. To raise

---

288. Dickens, Charles. *David Copperfield*, 1850
289. From *The Confessions of Isobel Gowdie*, Auldearne, Scotland 1662

the wind, the sailors must undo one or two knots depending on how much wind they need. Untying all three knots would cause a gale to blow.[290]

Selling the Wind drawing. The Museum of Witchcraft (No. 3036)

To Steal Milk from Your Neighbours

Make a rope of hairs from the tails of several cows, whose exact number was indicated by knots in the rope. While tugging at the rope repeat:

Cow's milk and mare's milk,
And every beast that bears milk,

---

290. The Museum of Witchcraft library & archives

Between St. Johnstone's and Dundee,
Come a' to me, come a' to me.[291]

The Hand of Glory ❧

Throughout this book there are many references to the use of various parts of human anatomy in magic spells, but possibly the strangest is the 'Hand of Glory'. This is the hand of an executed felon which is cut from the body and converted into a candle or candle holder. It seems that one can mount a candle in the palm of the hand or use the fingers as candle holders. The candle should be made from the fat (or tallow) of the same felon. Tradition has it that, carrying a lighted 'Hand of Glory' will temporarily prevent anyone in its proximity seeing, hearing or waking. Some accounts say that the lighted candle will also unlock any secured doors in its path. The appeal of this magical tool to burglars is obvious. As late as 1831, *'The Observer'* newspaper reported that, in Ireland, *'thieves attempted to commit a robbery on the estate of Mr.*

---

291. Lawrence, Robert. *The Magic Of The Horse-Shoe,* 1889

Nappe. They entered the house armed with a "Dead Man's Hand", with a lighted candle in it, believing that a candle placed in a dead man's hand will not be seen by any but those by whom it is used and that it will prevent those who may be asleep from awaking. The inmates however were alarmed, and the robbers fled, leaving the hand behind them'.[292]

We find details of how to prepare your Hand of Glory in an account from 1751: *'Take the hand, right or left, of a hanged person hanged and exposed on the highway; wrap it up in a piece of shroud or winding-sheet, in which let it be well squeezed, to get out any small quantity of blood that may have remained in it: then put it into an earthenware vessel with zimat, salt-peter, salt, and long pepper, the whole being well powdered: leave it for fifteen days in that vessel; afterwards take it out, and expose it to the noon tide sun in the dog-days, till it is thoroughly dry; and if the sun is not sufficient, put it into an oven heated with fern and vervain: then compose a kind of candle with fat from the hanged man, virgin wax, and sesame of Lapland. The hand of Glory is used as a candlestick to hold this*

---

292. Brant, John. *Observations on Popular Antiquities,* 1842

candle when lighted. Its properties are, that, wheresoever any one goes with this dreadful instrument, the persons to whom it is presented will be deprived of all power of motion.' [293]

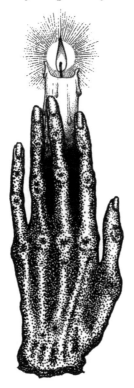

293. Magnus, Albertus. *Secrets Merveilleux de la Magie Naturelle et Cabalistique du Petit Albert*

Thomas Ingoldsby in his *'Ingoldsby Legends'* wrote:

Wherever that terrible light shall burn,
Vainly the sleeper may toss and turn;
His leaden eyes shall he ne'r unclose
So long as that magical taper glows,
Life and treasure shall he command
Who knoweth the charm of the glorious Hand.[294]

The 'Wondrous Candle' is a strange candle which is closely related to the 'Hand of Glory'. It was discovered amongst various other magical items in a secret loft space in Snowshill Manor in Gloucestershire. The room was decorated with alchemical paintings on the walls and a magic circle on the floor. The 'Witches Garret', as the room became known, is where the manor's eccentric owner, Charles Wade, placed his collection of magical objects and possibly practiced magic. In his notes, Wade describes how the candle is made of human tallow and, when lit, it makes the bearer invisible to others.

---

294. Ingoldsby, Thomas. *The Ingoldsby Legends*, 1837

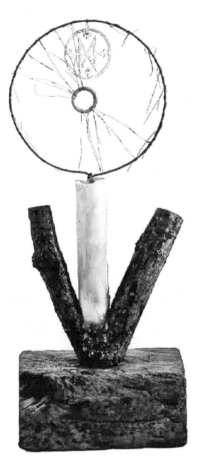

Charles Wade's Wonderous Candle.
The Museum of Witchcraft (No. 346)

Yet another method to render oneself invisible is described in the 1910 *'Book of Charms and Ceremonies':*

In January, in the day and hour of Saturn, make a small image of a man out of yellow wax. Suspend the said figure by one of your hairs from the vault of a cavern, at the hour of midnight, perfuming it with the proper incense, thou shall say:

'METATRON, MELEKH, BEROTH, NOTH, VENIBBETH, MACH, and all ye, I conjure thee, O Figure of Wax, that by the virtue of these words, thou render me invisible wherever I may bear thee with me. Amen'

And, having censed it anew, thou shall bury it in the same place in a small deal box, and any time that thou wishest to pass or enter into any place without being seen bear the figure in your left pocket and say:

'Come unto me, and never quit me whithersoever I shall go.'

Afterwards thou shalt take it carefully back unto the before-mentioned place, and cover it with earth until thou shalt need it again.[295]

---

295. *The Book of Charms and Ceremonies*, 1910

Whilst we do not know what *'the proper incense'* was in the spell, it probably included myrrh and henbane, as they are associated with Saturn. This charm is clearly derived from a slightly more complicated, but similar, ritual that appears in the 17th century *'The Key of Solomon.'*[296]

Vervain was valued by burglars as it would magically open locked doors. *'Gerard's Herbal'* (1597) warned against using the herb for *'witchard and sourcery'* and said that *'the Divell did reveal it as a secret and divine medicine'.*[297]

A Charm for Gathering Vervain

Before gathering Vervain for magical use, you should speak this charm:

All-hele, thou holy herb, Vervin,
Growing on the ground;
In the Mount of Calvary
There wast thou found;

296. Trans. Mathers, Macgregor. *The Key of Solomon the King (Clavicula Salomonis),* 1888
297. Howard, Michael. *A Witch's Herbal,* 2012

Thou helpest many a grief,
And stanchest many a wound.
In the name of sweet Jesus
I take thee from the ground.
O Lord, effect the same
That I do now go about.

And the following should be said when pulling the herb:

In the name of God, on Mount Olivet
First I found thee;
In the name of Jesus
I pull thee from the ground.[298]

To See Things Unseen by Others

You must take the green juice of the inner bark of a bourtree (elder tree) and apply it to the eyelids of a baptised person.[299]

To Discover a Thief

Collect as many small pebbles from a running stream as there are suspects to the theft. Take the pebbles to your

---

298. *Lancashire Folk-lore,*1882
299. McNeill, F. Marian. *The Silver Bough,* 1956

house, make them red-hot, and bury them under the main entrance to your house. After three days, dig them up after sunrise. Place a bowl of water in the middle of a circle in which there is a cross and the written words *'Christus vicit, Christus regnat, Christus imperrat'*. Throw the pebbles into the water, each one in the name of a suspect. The pebble associated with the thief will make the water boil.[300] Another traditional method of discovering a thief was by 'sieve and shears'. The method was to stick the points of the shears in the wood of the sieve, and let two persons support it, balanced upright, with their two fingers; then read the 50th psalm and ask Saint Peter and Saint Paul if A or B is the thief, naming all the persons you suspect. On naming the real thief the sieve will turn suddenly around.[301] This method of spell craft, was also popular for general divination and love magic.

---

300. *The Book of Witches*, 1908
301. Brant, John. *Observations on Popular Antiquities*, 1842

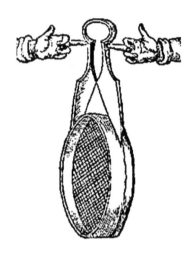

Theocritus wrote in c. 275BC;

A cunning woman she, I cross'd her hand she
turn'd to sieve and shears and told me true
That I should love, but not be lov'd by you.[302]

A Bible and key can also be used to discover a thief; place a key in the 50th psalm of The Bible and bind the book closed with a garter. The book is then suspended by a cord and the names

---

302. *The Third Idyll of Theocritus,* c. 275 BC

of suspects read out. The Bible and
key will spin when the thief's name is
announced.[303]

To Keep Treasures Hidden ✦

Hide them when the moon is in conjunction
with the sun and fume the place with coriander,
saffron, henbane, smallage, and black poppy,
of each a like quantity, bruised together, and
tempered with the juice of hemlock, that which
is so hid shall never be found, or taken away,
for the spirits governed by the sun and moon
will continually watch over the place; and if
anyone shall endeavour to take it away, he shall
be hurt by them, and shall fall into a frenzy.[304]

Health and safety warning; fuming
with black poppy, henbane, hemlock, etc,
can seriously damage your health and at
best it will give you a bad hangover!

To Find Buried Treasure ✦

We are told in a 16th century manuscript
to: *Make this figure following with the blade*
of a black whelpe and hang it about a white

---

303. Brant, John. *Observations on Popular Antiquities*, 1842
304. The Book of Charms and Ceremonies, 1910. p. 54

cocks neck and go there as the treasure is suspected and cast your cock out of your hand, and he shall go and stand right on it and crow. Dig there and take it out of the ground without any clarcke and your cock must have a cord or a line of seven yards long about his leg to have him again when you will – it is proven.[305]

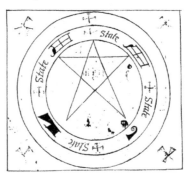

_____

305. Copy of 16th/17th century manuscript of magician's notes (once owned by Robert Lenkiewicz) held in The Museum of Witchcraft archive

To Get a Drink Within an Hour ✄

Say *'Crucifixus hoc signum vitam eternam. Amen'*.[306] This charm is from the confessions of James Device (1612) who was one of the ten 'Pendle Witches' hanged in 1612. Their story can be read in Joyce Froome's *'Wicked Enchantments'*.

To Make Holy Water & Bless a Church ✄

George Sinclair recorded in his book *'Satan's Invisible World Discovered'* (1685) that the *'Popish Clergy make their Holy Water by Charm or Conjuration thus:*

> *I conjure thee, thou Creature of Water in the name of the Father, Son, and Holy Ghost, that thou drive the Devil out of every corner of this church and Altar, so that he remain not within our Precinks, which are just and Holy.*[307]

This charm demonstrates how the writer, George Sinclair and others were keen to associate 17th century Catholicism with occult practices.

---

306. *Lancashire Folk-lore,*1882
307. Sinclair, George. *Satan's Invisible World Discovered,* 1685

To Seal or Conclude a Spell ✄

I wind, I bind,
This spell be mine! [308]

A song published in *'Songs of Love'* (1894) incorporates a version of this charm:

I wind, I bind, my true love to find,
So sang the maiden by the well;
I wind, I bind, my true love to find,
And thus she wrought the magic spell. [309]

The reference to *'the maiden by the well'* is interesting. Traditionally, holy wells are places for tying clouties (strips of cloth) to overhanging trees as a form of knot magic. Could the winding and binding in the charm be referring to the preparation and tying of a cloutie to a tree?

For Beauty ✄

For women to be more beautiful, and be protected from men, the following

---

308. The Museum of Witchcraft Library & Archives
309. T. Alcliffe Teske. *Songs of Love,* 1894

charm should be recited in early
summer under a waxing moon whilst
gathering yarrow:

I will pick the smooth yarrow
That my figure may be more elegant,
That my lips may be warmer,
That my voice may be more cheerful;
May my voice be like a sunbeam,
May my lips be like the juice of the strawberries,
May I be an island in the sea,
May I be a hill in the land
May I be a star when the moon wanes,
May I be a staff to the weak one;
I shall wound every man,
No man shall wound me.[310]

Health and safety notice; whilst
this spell grants the power to wound
every man I would advise against this
course of action (please)!

---

310. Pepper, Elizabeth. *Magic Spells & Incantations,* 2001

A Charm for Plucking Yarrow

I will pull the yarrow
As Mary pulled it with her two hands
I will pull it with my strength
I will pull it with the hollow of my hand.[311]

Young women were told to sew yarrow into a sachet and place it under their pillows to dream of a 'bosom friend' or lover.[312] Also see the charm *'To see your future lover'* that includes a yarrow plucking element.

A Charm for Pulling Pearlwort

I will pull the pearlwort
The plant that Christ ordained;
No fear has it of fire-burning,
Or wars of fairy woman.

Pearlwort had various magical uses, it was placed on the lintel of a door to prevent sluagh (troublesome spirits of the dead), or an 'arial host' entering. It was

---

311. McNeill, F. Marian. *The Silver Bough*, 1956
312. Howard, Michael. *A Witch's Herbal*, 2012

also placed on the right knee of a woman in labour to comfort and relieve her. It would protect new born children from the fairy woman who might substitute the child for a changeling.[313]

Relieve the Pain from One You Have Struck ✄
Spit into the middle of the hand with which you gave the blow, and the party that was smitten, whether he be near or far off, will be freed from pain.[314]

To Stop a Chimney Smoking ✄
Put a bottle in a smoking chimney. The recorder of this notes that the idea may have been taken from the psalms; *'I become like a bottle in the smoke'* (Psalm 119:83).[315]

Protection from Lightning-Strike ✄
To protect yourself, wear a chaplet or wreath of laurel about your neck, or a bay leaf about your person, or carry a seal skin. Or to protect your house from

313. McNeill, F. Marian. *The Silver Bough*, 1956
314. *The Book of Charms and Ceremonies*, 1910, p. 53
315. Havergal, F.T. *Herefordshire Words, Superstitions & Customs*, 1887

lightning, grow the herb housleek (houseleek), or syngreen on your roof, and hang the slough of an adder from the rafters, to protect it from fire.[316]

To Stop Wildfire

Speak this charm:

Christ he walketh over the land
Carried the wildfire in his hand
He rebuked the fire and bid it stand;
Stand, wildfire, stand
Stand, wildfire stand
Stand, wildfire stand
In the name of the Father, Son, and Holy Ghost.[317]

To Learn about a Troublesome Ghost

Reginald Scot, in 1584, gave us the following:

By the mysteries of the deep, by the flames of Banal, by the power of the east, and the silence of the night, by the holy rites of Hecate, I

316. Brant, John. *Observations on Popular Antiquities,* 1842, & Various authors, *Notes & Queries,* 1880
317. Couch, Jonathan. *The History of Polrerrow,* 1871

conjure and exorcise thee, thou distressed spirit, to present thyself here, and reveal unto me the cause of thy calamity, why thou didst offer violence to thy own liege life, where thou art now in being, and where thou wilt hereafter be.[318]

Such is the interest in this ritual that it has been reproduced in many subsequent influential books including Ebenezer Sibly's *'A New and Complete Illustration of the Occult Sciences'* 1758; *'The Book of Black Magic and of Pacts'* by Arthur Edward Waite 1910; and even *'The Royal Lady's Magazine'* 1832.

To Stop Gossip ⚕

Speak no evil, write no ill
May the tongue and hands be still
As I bind this is my will.[319]

For Sound Sleep ⚕

All honest people wishing to have sound sleep must keep the witches from their

---

318. Scot, Reginald. *The Discovery of Witchcraft*, 1584
319. The Museum of Witchcraft Library & Archives

beds by having a branch of wiggen (rowan) at their bed-head.[320]

To Become a Witch ✎

In April and May 1662, Isobel Gowdie was examined by John Innes, notary public in Auldearne. The depositions state that they were given voluntarily, *'without any compulsitorris…or pressure'* (i.e. without torture). Isobel Gowdie confessed that she met the devil and renounced her baptism putting one of her hands *'to the crown of my head and the other to the sole of my foot and renounced all betwixt my two hands to the Devil'*. It must be born in mind that Gowdie may have been offered leniency if she confessed.

This method of initiation is also mentioned in a 1685 publication that contains transcripts of the trial of Annabil Stewart of Paisly in the Scottish lowlands who was enticed by her mother (who promised her a new coat) to *'put one hand to the crown of her head and the other to the sole of her foot, and did give up her self sole and body to the devil…the devil in the shape of a black man lay*

---

320. *Lancashire Folk-lore,*1882

with her in the bed, under the cloaths…she found him cold.' [321]

Another version from the Shetland Islands explains that when the moon is at midnight, the aspirant must go to the seashore and lie down upon the beach below the tidemark. She must then put her left hand under the soles of her feet, the right hand on the top of her head, and repeat three times: *'The muckel maister Deil tak what's atween dis twa hands!*

Image from Joseph Glanvil's *Saducismus Triumphatus*

321. Sinclair, George. *Satan's Invisible World Discovered,* 1685

The Devil will then appear and clinch the bargain by shaking hands! [322]

The initiation ritual is also described and illustrated (see previous page) in Glanvil's *'Saducismus Triumphatus'* 1681.

A Charm for a Dying Person ❧

The mist the dew,
The dew the mist,
The mist the dew
In the eye of my love
In the eye of my love
Thou who didst open the young eye,
Close it tonight in the sleep of death,
In the sleep of death.[323]

This touching death croon from the isle of Eigg in Scotland was chanted over a dying person. The croon would be chanted by the soul-friend or a village elder who would sometimes be accompanied by helpers. Until recently, it was an important and common practice

---

322. McNeill, F. Marian. The Silver Bough, 1956
323. Macleod, Kenneth. *The Road to The Isles,* 1927

to chant over dying villagers to ensure their safe journey to an afterlife.

To Ease a Person's Death ✄

Place salt in a church paten (a plate used to carry the bread at the Eucharist), and place it on the breast of the dying person.[324]

This unusual charm was collected in Charlcombe, near Bath in 1852.

For Success in Battle ✄

Around the year 1600, a soldier lost his magic talisman in an East Anglian field. Four hundred years later, metal detectorist Bill Lovett, found it 18inches beneath the ground. The magic square of Mars, and all the sigils and spirit names inscribed on this lovely old object clearly indicate that it was intended to ensure success in battle and to prevent bleeding. But what a dilemma the wearer must have faced because, in 1600, the use of magical talismans and amulets such as this was illegal and punishable by death.

---

324. Various authors, Notes & Queries, 1855

Mars Talisman. Museum of Witchcraft (No. 2741)

To Help With All Magical Work ⚜

Sing or chant the following charm:

> *Fire flame and fire burn*
> *Make the mill of magic turn*
> *Work the will for which I pray*
> *Io, Dio, Ha, He Yay!*

Air breath and air blow,
Make the mill of magic go
Work the will for which I pray
Io, Dio, Ha, He Yay!

Water heat and water boil
Make the mill of magic toil
Work the will for which I pray
Io, Dio, Ha, He Yay!

Earth without and earth within
Make the mill of magic spin
Work the will for which I pray
Io, Dio, Ha, He Yay! [325]

Or say:

By Robin son of Art,
And our Good Lady of the Moon
By the sun that shines for us,
By all the stars that look down on us,
Grant me my will,
So mote it be. [326]

---

325. The Museum of Witchcraft Library & Archives
326. *Ibid*

To Gain a Woman ✤

Put a frog into a pot that is full of holes and 'stop it fast'. Walking against the wind, approach a crossroads and bury the pot in an anthill and leave it there for nine days. Then collect your frog and place the remaining bones in running water and one bone will float upstream. Set this bone in a ring. Any woman touched with the ring 'shall never resist till she hath been with ye'.[327]

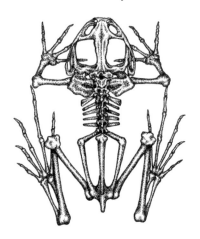

---

327. Copy of 16th/17th century manuscript of magician's notes (once owned by Robert Lenkiewicz) held in The Museum of Witchcraft archive

To Invoke Joy ✢
Chant the following:

Cantil o, Cantil ee!
Joy to all thee gone before
Whose longer stay had pleased us
Cantil o, Cantil ee!

Joy to all thee left behind
Whose leaving would have grieved us.
Cantil o, Cantil ee!
Joy to all thee still to come
Whose song may lift the weary.
Cantil o, Cantil ee! [328]

---

328. Macleod, Kenneth. *The Road to The Isles*, 1927

The Cocke (Cock) Rock.
Museum of Witchcraft (No.1018)

A Parting Thought

I do hope that in a hundred years time, someone writing a book on British folklore will stumble across this publication and 'steal' some of its secrets. It is only through the publication and republication of these lovely old spells and charms that they will survive. Whilst there are still pellars, charmers, witches and wise women practicing their magical arts, few of them still use the old ways and those who do are often ridiculed and marginalised. Sadly I don't believe we can depend on the ancestral tradition of 'the passing on' of spells and charms to the next generations to keep the magic alive. A letter which accompanied an object on display in the Museum of Witchcraft reads:

Please find enclosed the Cocke Rock which has been in my family's possession for many generations. My Grandmother told me that, as late as the 1920s, women wishing to conceive would put the stone under their pillow on the night of the full moon and they were guaranteed to be 'with child' within nine months. I am sending this to you anonymously partly because no one in my village now believes in its powers and also because I feel that your museum is the best resting place for it and I don't want to start more gossip among the younger 'come-latelys' in the community. Please look after the stone.

How very sad that few people seem to believe in magic any more, and that yet one more family tradition has died. In recent years, I have been delighted to witness a revival of interest in British folk culture. Youngsters are singing and dancing our fabulous traditional songs and dances with pride. Touch wood, in years to come, there will also be a revival of interest in our spells and charms and people will once again realise that we live in a land full of magical traditions.

Flags Flax Fodder and Frig
Merry Meet and Merry Part

Bibliography & Resources

Agrippa. *De Occulta Philosophia*, 1533

Anon. *The Most Wonderfull & True Storie*, 1597

Aubrey, John. *Remaines of Gentilisme & Judaisme*, 1686-87

Barrett, Francis. *The Magus*, 1801

Bateson, J.K. *Moorland Mysteries*, 1925

Brant, John. *Observations on Popular Antiquities*, 1842

Bromhall, Thomas. *A Treaties of Specters*, 1658

Carmichael, Alexander. *Carmina Gadelica*, 1900

Chambers, Robert. *Popular Rhymes, Fireside Stories, & Amusements of Scotland*, 1842

Child, Francis James. *The English & Scottish Popular Ballads*, 1882-1898

Cielo, Astra. *Signs Omens & Superstitions*, 1918

Copy of 16th/17th century manuscript of magician's notes, once owned by Robert Lenkiewicz, held in The Museum of Witchcraft archive

Couch, Jonathan. *The History of Polperro,*1871

Davidson, Thomas. *Rowan Tree & Red Thread*, 1949

Davies, Dr. Owen. *Popular Magic: Cunning Folk in English History*, 2007

Witchcraft, Magic & Culture, 1736-1951, 1999

Devon & Cornwall Notes & Queries, Vol. 6, 1911

Devonshire Association Folk-Lore Transactions, 1862 -1928

Dickens, Charles. *David Copperfield,* 1850

Frome, Joyce. *Wicked Enchantments,* 2010

Glanville. *Saducismus Trimphatus,* 1681

Glyde Junior, John. *The New Suffolk Garland,* 1866

    The Norfolk Garland, 1872

Graves, Robert. *The White Goddess*

Gray, William G. *Magical Ritual Methods,* 1971

Havergal, F.T. *Herefordshire Words, Superstitions & Customs,* 1887. Reprinted by Oakleaf Books in 2001

Henderson, William. *Notes on the Folk-Lore of the Northern Counties of England and the Borders,* 1879

Hewett, Sarah. *The Peasant Speech of Devon,* 1892

Hole, Christina. *English Folklore,* 1940

Howard, Michael. *A Witch's Herbal,* 2012

    The Cauldron Magazine, 1976-2015

Ingoldsby, Thomas. *The Ingoldsby Legends,* 1837

Jones, K. I. (Ed.) *Folklore & Witchcraft of Devon & Cornwall,* 1997

Kinsman, John. *The Cornish Handbook,* 1931

Lancashire Folk-lore, 1882 (As reprinted in facsimile in *Lancashire Witchcraft, Charms and Spells* by Oakmagic Publications in 2002)

Lawrence, Robert. *The Magic Of The Horse-Shoe,* 1889

Leyland, Charles. *Gypsy Sorcery & Fortune Telling,* 1891

Lovett, Edward. *Magic in Modern London,* 1925 (Reprinted with additional material in 2014 by Red Thread Books)

Macleod, Kenneth. *The Road to The Isles,* 1927

Magical Charms Potions & Secrets for Love, 1972

Magnus, Albertus. *Secrets Merveilleux de la Magie Naturelle et Cabalistique du Petit Albert*

    The Petit Albert, 1722

McNeill, F. Marian. *The Silver Bough,* 1956

Moore, Thomas. *The Treasury of Botany,* 1866

News from Scotland, trial pamphlet, 1591

Oakmagic. *The Cornish Antiquary,* 2002

Old Cornwall (various papers). Republished by Oakmagic in *Folklore & Witchcraft of the Cornish Village,* 2004

Pepper, Elizabeth. *Magic Spells & Incantations,* 2001

Pitcairn, Robert. *Criminal Trials in Scotland,* 1833

Richard Flecknoe's Diarium, 1658

Roper, Jonathan. *English Verbal Charms*

Scot, Reginald. *The Discovery of Witchcraft,* 1584

Semmens, Jason. *The Cornish Witch Finder*

Sibly, Ebenezer. *A New & Complete Illustration of the Occult Sciences,* 1758

Sinclair, George. *Satan's Invisible World Discovered,* 1685

Somerset & Dorset *Notes & Queries*

Songs of Witchcraft & Magic. (CD) The Museum of Witchcraft

Sykes, Wirt. *British Goblins*, (1881)

T. Alcliffe Teske. *Songs of Love*, 1894

The Book of Charms and Ceremonies, 1910

The Book of Witches, 1908

The Daily Jouurnal, 1731

The Folk-Lore Record, 1882

The Gentleman's Magazine, 1810

The Museum of Witchcraft library & archives, Boscastle, Cornwall UK

The Third Idyll of Theocritus, c 275 BC

The Weekly Mercury, 1883

Thiselton Dyer, T.F. *English Folklore*, 1880 (Reprints from *The Western Antiquary*, 1883 -1884 and Devon & Cornwall *Notes & Queries*.)

Transactions of the Penzance Natural History & Antiquarian Society, 1888. Republished by Oakmagic in *Folklore & Witchcraft of the Cornish Village*, 2004

Trans. Mathers, Macgregor. *The Key of Solomon the King (Clavicula Salomonis)*, 1888

Various authors, *Notes & Queries*, 1855 & 1880

Wright, R.A. *English Folklore*, 1928

Index

Lightning Source UK Ltd.
Milton Keynes UK
UKHW020015120122
396991UK00005B/32

9 781909 602175